REPORT FROM
AFGHANISTAN

ALSO BY GÉRARD CHALIAND

— Armed Struggle in Africa
— The Peasants of North Vietnam
— The Palestinian Resistance
— Revolution in the Third World:
  Myths and Prospects
— People Without a Country:
  The Kurds and Kurdistan (editor)
— Food Without Frontiers
— The Struggle for Africa: Great Power Strategies
— Guerrilla Strategies: An Historical Anthology
  from the Long March to Our Days (editor)

GÉRARD CHALIAND

REPORT FROM AFGHANISTAN

TRANSLATED BY TAMAR JACOBY

THE VIKING PRESS • NEW YORK
PENGUIN BOOKS

Soc
DS
371.2
C4613
1982

Penguin Books Ltd, Harmondsworth,
Middlesex, England
Penguin Books, 625 Madison Avenue,
New York, New York 10022, U.S.A.
Penguin Books Australia Ltd, Ringwood,
Victoria, Australia
Penguin Books Canada Limited, 2801 John Street,
Markham, Ontario, Canada L3R 1B4
Penguin Books (N.Z.) Ltd, 182–190 Wairau Road,
Auckland 10, New Zealand

This translation first published in 1982 in hardcover and paperback editions by The Viking Press and
Penguin Books, 625 Madison Avenue, New York, N.Y. 10022
Published simultaneously in Canada

Portions of this book appeared originally in *The New York Review of Books*, in different form.

Grateful acknowledgment is made to *Esprit*, Paris, for permission to reprint a selection from Olivier
Roy's article entitled "Afghanistan: la 'révolution' par le vide," which appeared in the May 1980
issue of *Esprit*.

LIBRARY OF CONGRESS CATALOGING IN PUBLICATION DATA
Chaliand, Gérard, 1934–
    Report from Afghanistan.
    Translation of: Rapport sur la résistance
afghane.
    Includes index.
    1. Afghanistan—History—Soviet Occupation,
1979– .   I. Title.
DS371.2.C4613   958'.1044   81-21963
ISBN 0-670-59473-3 (hardbound)   AACR2
ISBN 0 14 00.6516 4 (paperbound)

Printed in the United States of America
Set in Times Roman and Helvetica Light

ACKNOWLEDGMENTS

I want to thank warmly Tamar Jacoby, who did a remarkable job in translating my book, and, as ever, my editor, Elisabeth Sifton, for her proficiency and expertise. I am also happy once again to thank Robert Silvers, of *The New York Review of Books,* who published sections of this book.

HISTORICAL MAP

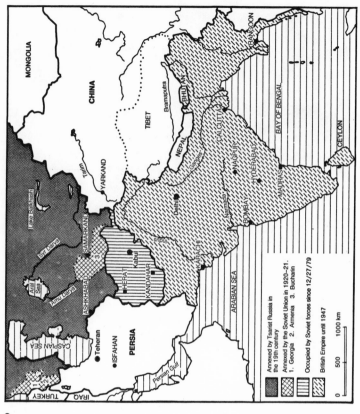

Annexed by Tsarist Russia in the 19th century

Annexed by the Soviet Union in 1920–21.
1. Georgia 2. Armenia 3. Bucharin

Occupied by Soviet forces since 12/27/79

British Empire until 1947

0   500   1000 km

TERRAIN OF AFGHANISTAN

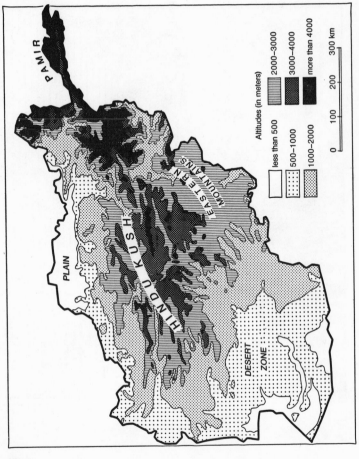

Altitudes (in meters)

less than 500
500–1000
1000–2000
2000–3000
3000–4000
more than 4000

0   100   200   300 km

PAMIR

HINDU KUSH

EASTERN MOUNTAINS

PLAIN

DESERT ZONE

POPULATION

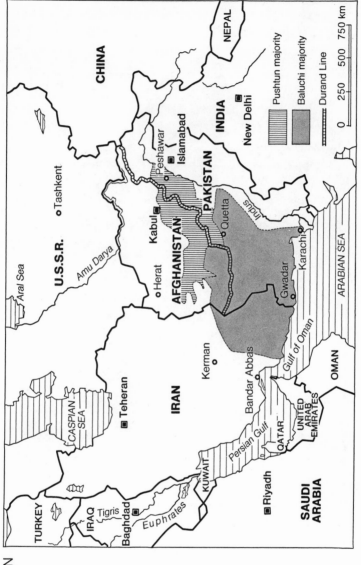

ETHNIC DISTRIBUTION

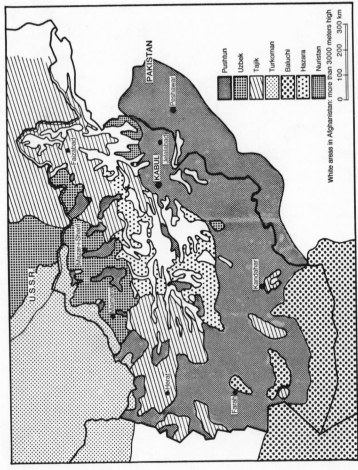

Pushtun

Uzbek

Tajik

Turkoman

Baluchi

Hazara

Nuristan

White areas in Afghanistan: more than 3000 meters high

0   100   200   300 km

PAKISTAN

Peshawar

Faizabad

KABUL
Jelalabad

Mazar-i-Sharif

Maimana

U.S.S.R.

Kandahar

Herat

Farah

SOVIET PRESENCE

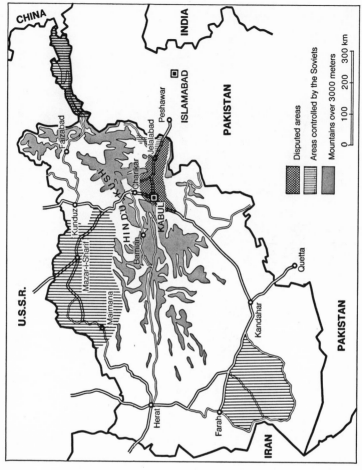

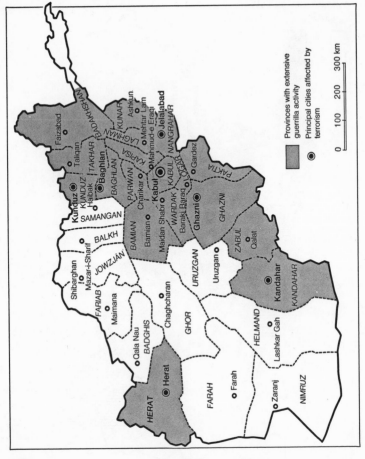

GUERRILLA AND
TERRORIST ACTIVITY

Provinces with extensive
guerrilla activity

Principal cities affected by
terrorism

0   100   200   300 km

Never, under any circumstances, is Soviet foreign policy designed to torpedo *détente*. Soviet aid to Afghanistan in no way interferes with *détente*. The Soviet Union acted in full compliance with the UN charter, responding to a request by the Afghan government, and bringing aid to a country that had been the victim of aggression. Since when, one wonders then, has it been true that aggression does not aggravate a situation, while the response to that aggression does aggravate it?

Boris Ponomarev, Secretary of the Communist Party
of the Soviet Union,
December 3, 1980

If the Great Soviet Union had not given its heroic aid to Afghanistan, there would be no free, revolutionary, independent, and nonaligned Afghanistan in existence today.

Babrak Karmal, in a speech to the 26th
Congress of the Communist Party of the Soviet Union,
February 25, 1981

CONTENTS

REPORT FROM
AFGHANISTAN

1 INTRODUCTION

The city of Peshawar, in northern Pakistan, is the headquarters of the half-dozen organizations that make up the exiled Afghan resistance movement. It is a middle-sized city without particular charm, set in a large, flat valley. Most of the population belong to an ethnic group called "Pathan" in Pakistan and "Pushtun" across the border in Afghanistan. These people were first divided by the British colonial government that administered the region at the time of the Indian empire. The frontier that has separated Afghan from Pakistani Pushtuns since the end of the nineteenth century is called the Durand line, named for the British official who drew it, Sir Mortimer Durand. Like many boundaries drawn through mountainous regions, it passes along the crests of the hills. The Pathan region of Pakistan is still called by the name the British gave it: North-West Frontier Province (N.W.F.P.).

Peshawar boasts no special monuments and only one museum, filled with minor works, but in the old city there is a merchants' quarter where virtually any kind of Pakistani ar-

tisan or small shopkeeper can be found. The finish on artisans' work almost always leaves something to be desired—
perfection exists only in nature—but Peshawar craftsmen
have recently learned to make the handsome Bukhara rugs,
now produced in Afghanistan as well as in the U.S.S.R., and
they make fine silver jewelry set with semiprecious stones
such as lapis lazuli.

The British, French, and Americans maintain cultural cen-
ters in Peshawar, the American one guarded by the police
since the anti-American riots of December 1979. They are lo-
cated in the neighborhood of Harbab Road, the modern
commercial street where the office of Pakistani International
Airlines, the city's biggest cinema, and three bookstores are
also found. After visiting the souk in the old city, tourists are
perhaps most surprised by the bookstores in Peshawar, which
are better in quality than the bookstores in many Western
cities. They not only sell English translations of the major
works of Oriental and Western literature, but also reprint
editions of many classical works concerning Afghanistan,
Pakistan, and India—works like an account of the voyage
that Mountstuart Elphinstone made *Of the Kingdom of Cabul*
early in the nineteenth century. A British agent and perceptive observer, Elphinstone was sent to Afghanistan on an
exploratory mission, to report on a Napoleonic scheme to
sabotage the British land route to India. The scheme was
never executed, and after 1815, the threat disappeared. But
Elphinstone was also a distinguished writer and has left us an
important book, unmatched by anything of its kind.

The British soon had another rival in the region: the Russian empire. And in the bookstores of Peshawar one finds
many works written by British adventurers who came to
Afghanistan in the service of the state—a more common sort
of adventurer than the solitary gentlemen who traveled in

Central Asia on their own. One such British agent was Sir Alexander Burnes, who published in Paris in 1835 a four-volume account of his *Voyages à l'embouchure de l'Indus à Lahore, Caboul, Belkh et à Boukhara et retour par la Perse* ("Travels to the Mouth of the Indus to Lahore, Kabul, Balkh and to Bukhara, Returning by Way of Persia"). Another was C. Masson, who published in London in 1842 a three-volume *Narrative of Various Journeys in Balouchistan, Afghanistan and the Punjab.* One can also find the memoirs of Babur, the great conqueror, who founded the Moghul empire in the six-teenth century. Overwhelmed by the monsoon in his new capital Delhi, he wrote: "Nothing is more beautiful than Kabul. Its air is irreplaceable. . . ."

Peshawar is a sprawling city, built almost entirely of one-story houses. The best way to cross the city is by taxi-scooter—a small vehicle with two narrow seats, usually painted in the gaudy colors found on buses and trucks. It is usually enough to tell the driver the name of the Afghan or-ganization you want to visit and the neighborhood where it has its headquarters to be driven off at great speed, through dusty streets, accompanied by the sound of countless horns.

The offices of the Afghan organizations are usually modest. At the entrance, there is often a crowd: a guard summarily searches the Afghans waiting there but allows foreigners—usually Westerners—to enter freely. Inside, a number of fighters sit, waiting, with nothing to do. No training is given to them, no particular discipline maintained—although the headquarters are generally neat and the toilets always clean.

It was not easy, for me at least, to enter Afghanistan. Four times on my first visit in 1980 I was disappointed by the false promises of the movements or groups I contacted. The Is-lamic Society of Afghanistan promised me a long tour of Ba-dakhshan province, near the Soviet border. I spent two nights

[handwritten margin note, right: description of peshawar]

[handwritten margin note, left: 1st trip no successful]

at the movement's headquarters, chatting with young Uzbeks and Turkomen. (They spoke their own language and I answered in Turkish, and we managed a simple conversation.) At dawn on the third morning the group left Peshawar, and I did not discover until midday that it would not be possible for me to make my way alone from Chitral in northern Pakistan, where I had agreed to rejoin the guides. Then the movement led by Mohamedi Harakat was supposed to come find me the next day and take me to Paktia province. I waited in vain. I spent another futile morning from six to eleven o'clock waiting with my occasional companion, the British photographer Peter Juvenal, at the headquarters of the generally reputable Islamic Party led by Yunis Khalis. Their guides had agreed to lead a group of journalists from a West German magazine across the border into Afghanistan, and so could not take any other observers. Lastly, I arranged to meet the next day at six in the morning with a group organized by Abdel Rauf, a former Afghan army officer who was famous throughout the country for having taken arms, troops, and baggage with him when he deserted from the regular army. (The weapons were later confiscated by the Islamic Party of Gulbudin Hekmatyar.) At ten o'clock he still had not appeared.

My fifth attempt was successful, thanks to Amin Wardak, a member of S. A. Gailani's National Front for Islamic Revolution. And four months later, in the autumn of 1980, when I made my second trip across the border into Afghanistan, I had a number of reliable contacts, and had no trouble at all finding a guide in Peshawar.

All the resistance organizations ask observers entering Afghanistan to dress like traditional Afghanis: for the men, billowing trousers and long shirt reaching to the knees, and either a Pushtun turban or a Nuristani hat called a *pakul*. They also ask that you grow a mustache.

One approaches the Afghan border by bus or in a taxi. The road passes through the so-called tribal zones where it is forbidden to travel after nightfall, and en route there are half a dozen road blocks manned by Pakistani police. It is usually easy enough to pass through the check points. Since no one has papers, even in the most extreme instances the police can do little more than enter the bus to examine the faces, and sometimes the packages, of a few of the passengers.

The last night in Pakistan is spent in a frontier town, and in the morning, at dawn, one leaves clandestinely to cross the border on foot. There is nothing surprising about the appearance of the Afghan mujahedeen: their costume and their rough highlander's faces are familiar enough from photographs, as is the stunning alpine landscape of the country's central and western regions.

You rarely feel alone on the steep trails that cross this terrain, usually looking down on streams of more or less drinkable water, since you frequently pass other groups of mujahedeen. Each wears a large, crested Pushtun turban or a low hat with a rolled brim, a long shirt, and some kind of vest. A bullet-studded bandolier, slung across the shoulder, holds in place the characteristic straight Pushtun dagger. Most Afghans are good walkers, and the daily march is often as long as ten hours. As a result, there is little time left in the day to observe guerrilla activity at first hand.

We occasionally stopped at small earthen tea houses called *tchai khane,* which serve both green Chinese tea and black India tea—a simple emblem of Afghanistan's place at a crossroads of trade between east and west. Both kinds of tea are drunk with lots of sugar, which helps to prevent dehydration and loss of energy. Although Afghanistan is far from the poorest country on the Indian subcontinent, most Afghans live on very little. A typical meal consists of unleavened bread dipped in sauce and perhaps some yoghurt. There are no fruits or vegetables and meat is rare. One usually spends the night in a camp built by mujahedeen or in a village; where fighters are generally treated with hospitality.

Guerrilla warfare is a relatively monotonous activity, nothing like what it is shown to be in movies or novels. It consists mainly of walking—pleasant enough as exercise but hardly spectacular. You visit rebel camps and villages, you hide, and you eat and drink whatever you can—in the Kunar province, nothing but tea and unleavened bread. From time to time you are shelled by the enemy and occasionally you participate in an ambush, but rarely in a prolonged battle and hardly ever in an assault. However confusing a conventional battle may seem to a given soldier or observer, it is at least confined to a particular location and most of the time has clearly defined consequences. But to observe guerrilla warfare is to find yourself everywhere and nowhere, witness to a particularly fragmented reality. It helps a great deal if you can rely, in your evaluation of a resistance movement, not only on what you observe in the field and on whatever information from other witnesses that you are able to verify, but also on an accumulated knowledge of other guerrilla struggles.

For my part, I have spent nearly ten years in Asia, Africa, and Latin America, often in rural areas where social and political problems are particularly acute. In the course of these travels, I have been drawn by both taste and circumstances to study the armed struggles of several national liberation movements. I first spent time among guerrilla fighters in the early 1960s, in the aftermath of the Algerian war. I knew many representatives of the national liberation movements that grew up in the anticolonial climate after the war, particularly the leader Amilcar Cabral. So in 1964 I visited several training camps of the PAIGC (African Party for the Independence of Guinea and Cape Verde); in May and June 1966 I visited the resistance in Guinea-Bissau; in 1967 I spent two months in North Vietnam studying regional organization in villages along the Tonkin Gulf during the American bombing; in 1968 I went to Colombia to evaluate the guerrilla forces fighting in the rural areas there; I visited the Middle East several times in 1968–70, and spent time with several Palestinian groups in Jordan and Lebanon, including Fatah, the Popular Front for the Liberation of Palestine, and N. Hawatmeh's Democratic and Popular Front of Palestine; most recently, I have been in Eritrea, with the Popular Liberation Front of Eritrea, and in Iran with the Democratic Party of Iranian Kurdistan.

This report reflects two visits I made to Afghanistan, to Paktia and Kunar provinces, and to Peshawar, first in June and then in October and November 1980.

Whether one belongs to the right or the left, it is reassuring to interpret the world with certain preconceived schemas. And in the Third World particularly, people are given to Manichean visions of history and international conspiracy: the American imperialist conspiracy of the CIA, the Pentagon, and the military-industrial complex, led by multinational corporations; or the conspiracy of liberation movements controlled by the Soviet Union, determined to spread instability throughout the Third World.

The Soviet regime is without doubt the bloodiest and most deceptive caricature in modern history, a cruel parody of the ideas that supposedly inspire it. Notwithstanding its commitment to "the people," it oppresses countless peoples both within and beyond its borders. And yet in Africa, Asia, and Latin America, national liberation movements devoted to ending colonial and semicolonial domination generally find that the Soviet Union is on their side, while the liberal democracies of the West have almost always during the past three decades been on the side of oppression in the Third World. One has only to think of the two Vietnamese wars, the French and the American, of the Algerian war, and of the support that the United States and most NATO countries gave to the fascist Portuguese regime that fought for a decade to maintain colonies in Angola, Mozambique, and Guinea-Bissau. Nothing is ever as simple as it seems.

Throughout modern history, national independence has been seen as a principle worth defending. Not that the concept of a nation-state is a particularly encouraging one: after all, it has been at the root of countless cruel conflicts and is invariably used to justify the oppression of minorities. Still, it goes without saying today that peoples have the right to govern themselves: that much is assumed, on paper at least, as in the charter of the United Nations. In Afghanistan, this right of self-determination has evidently been violated by the U.S.S.R. After all, who but the most docile clients of Moscow would claim that the Afghan head of state, Hafizullah Amin, really asked the Russians to enter Kabul—only to be killed by them and replaced by his rival, Babrak Karmal?

Some historians defend the Soviet policy, conceived in the 1920s and pursued by Stalin, that has meant carving up the Muslim heart of Central Asia even against the wishes of local revolutionary leaders. In such a colonial setting, it is argued, modernization inevitably entailed some degree of subjugation. But that was another epoch, a different setting. Should the same thing happen again today, for the good of Afghanistan? Only those who are willing to pay any price for modernization that leads to "progress" can answer "yes" to that question.

Unlike most countries in Africa and Asia, Afghanistan has never been colonized. Like Yemen and Ethiopia, Afghanistan outside of Kabul remains astoundingly traditional: it hardly knows the shantytowns and other distortions that are commonplace in most dislocated Third World societies. For better or worse, as frustrated and underdeveloped as the Khalq faction was, this Marxist-Leninist group, which ruled Afghanistan in 1978–79 until the Soviet invasion, wanted to create a modern society by means of social revolution. Ironically enough this was also the goal of the rival Parcham faction, another Marxist-Leninist group, which the Soviet troops brought to power. That is why Afghan communists claim that history and progress are on their side while, according to them, the resistance will bring only reaction and obscurantism.

It is hard to argue with that claim, and it is certainly true that Soviet regions of Muslim Central Asia are more modern and better developed than Afghanistan is. As for the argument that Afghanistan should remain a kind of traditional ethnic preserve, such an alternative hardly seems plausible now that change has already begun.

But whatever the contradictions and ambiguities of the Afghan resistance movements, there is no denying the legitimacy of their fight against a destiny imposed by foreign tanks, whether in the name of "socialism" or "progress."

The Soviet invasion of Afghanistan in December 1979 marks a turning point: it was the first time in the years following World War II that Russian troops entered a country that does not belong to the Warsaw Pact.

Now for the first time since the middle of the nineteenth

century, Afghanistan is no longer a buffer state: Soviet troops guard the Pakistani border, only a few hundred kilometers from the Indian Ocean, and have a significant presence on Iran's western flank. The invasion may initially have been a defensive measure, a local maneuver designed to prevent the collapse of a socialist experiment in Afghanistan and replace a weak regime with an apparently hardier one. But no event in Afghanistan is without consequences for the rest of Central Asia, and the intervention has significantly shifted the geopolitical balance there. The U.S.S.R. entered Afghanistan at a crucial moment, when Pakistan was extremely vulnerable and Iran was caught up in an unpredictable transition. Clearly, Moscow is in a better position today than yesterday to influence events throughout the region, whether directly or indirectly.

The Soviet intervention was triggered by events within Afghanistan, but it cannot be explained without considering the international climate that made it possible. The 1970s were an important decade for both the United States and the Soviet Union. Moscow strengthened its military arsenal, while the Americans suffered political defeat in Vietnam, followed by the humiliation of the Watergate scandal. This permitted the Soviet Union and its Cuban ally to move into "power vacuums" like Angola and Ethiopia in the Third World. The fall of the Shah upset the balance of power in the Middle East, and when the hostages were taken at the U.S. embassy in Teheran, Washington found that it was paralyzed. Thus, no matter what happened inside Afghanistan, a Soviet intervention would not have been thinkable before the fall of the Shah and the blow it dealt to an America still recovering from defeat in Vietnam.

Although President Carter's foreign policy—in the Middle

East, in Africa, and in Latin America—was not in the end so disastrous as it seemed to many at the time, the President seems never to have fully grasped the real nature of relations between America and Russia. Carter hoped above all to reduce the tension between the two countries: he gave priority to arms control, nuclear nonproliferation, and human rights; but, preoccupied with nuclear defense, his administration neglected the conventional arms race. Russia took advantage of this and made considerable military gains throughout the world, largely compensating for the bitter defeat it suffered in Egypt when its personnel were expelled by President Anwar Sadat in 1972.

Since the Cuban missile crisis in 1962, the Soviet Union has steadily developed its global military strength, in both conventional and nuclear weapons. Since 1971, Moscow has been much concerned with the development of amicable relations between the United States and China, and has taken steps to resist "encirclement." And in the Third World, Soviet officials have shown remarkable tactical skill and long-range logistical planning. Thus the Soviet Union has become a world power—a position it did not command when Nixon and Kissinger held sway in Washington, when most Americans reassured themselves that the Soviet Union was only a regional power.

In this new geopolitical setting, it is extraordinarily difficult for the United States to respond effectively to each of the varied crises—in Ethiopia, Iran, and Afghanistan. In Iran the revolution was a response to that country's rapid modernization, while recent shifts of power in Ethiopia and Afghanistan were efforts to break out of what might be called social stagnation. All three upheavals have significant implications for the rivalry between East and West, but the roots of both the crises and their resolutions lie in particular domestic conditions. That is why the United States has not been able to maintain international stability by stubbornly supporting the social status quo in these conflicted countries.

2 THE AFGHAN SETTING

Afghanistan sits at the crossroads, historical and geographical, of three cultural worlds: the Middle East, with its Arab and Persian peoples; Central Asia, populated by Turks and Mongolians; and the Indian subcontinent. It has traditionally been a place that other peoples cross on their way to China. In ancient times, Alexander the Great passed through, and in the late first century A.D., Greek influence combined with Buddhist traditions to give rise to Gandharan art. In the middle of the seventh century, Islam spread into Afghanistan, leaving indelible marks. But the single most important influence was Persian culture—the model for the most distinguished and powerful Afghan dynasties, the Ghaznavid empire, which flourished from the tenth to the twelfth centuries. The Mongolians overran the country during the thirteenth century when they swept through the rest of Asia. During the fifteenth and sixteenth centuries, the Persian Safavid dynasty fought with Indian Moghul rulers for control of Afghanistan.

Then, in 1747, the Pushtun leader Ahmad Shah Durani proclaimed himself king at Kandahar, establishing the last Afghan empire—the foundation of the modern Afghan state consolidated by Abdur Rahman Khan, during his rule from 1880 to 1901.* The nineteenth century brought a series of civil wars as well as two British attempts, in 1839 and 1878, to impose imperial control. Afghans met the first invading column with fierce resistance, and the British defeat soon became legendary.

These futile British attempts to penetrate Afghanistan were enough to dissuade the Russians from trying anything similar, although in the second half of the nineteenth century Russia did advance as far as the Oxus River, now called the Amu Darya, which forms the border between Russia and Afghanistan. But when modern Afghanistan was created at the end of the nineteenth century, it was as a buffer state—the result of a compromise between Tsarist Russia and the British empire.

These two foreign powers traced the borders of Afghanistan in such a way that their empires, separated by an anomalous strip called the Wakhan Corridor, would not touch at any point. At the same time, the Pushtun Amir Abdur Rahman Khan was unifying the country under his control. Before he came to power in 1880, the country was divided into several regions: the area north of the Hindu Kush mountains and east of Herat was known as Turkistan; Kabulistan stretched south from the Hindu Kush to the Indus River; while the region farther south and southwest was known as Zabulistan. Abdur Rahman Khan brought them

---

* A. de Gardane, *Mission du général Gardane en Perse sous le premier Empire* (Paris, 1856).

together under his jurisdiction, conquering their different ethnic groups and tribal chiefs in a series of campaigns. He also brought Islam to the "kafirs," or infidels, of Nuristan.

The British contrived to control Afghan foreign policy until 1919, when a third Anglo-Afghan war freed Afghanistan from foreign domination. Then, from 1919 to 1979, Afghans enjoyed sixty years of independence and neutrality—a time of largely unsuccessful efforts to modernize and develop the country.

The 650,000 square kilometers of Afghanistan are sliced from east to west by the Hindu Kush, a mountainous barrier with peaks as high as 4000–5000 meters which stretches more than a thousand kilometers long and is 250 kilometers wide; it is crossed by a series of passes that run from north to south. In the northeast corner of Afghanistan the Hindu Kush gives way to the Pamir Mountains, with peaks as high as 7500 meters; these run through the Wakhan Corridor, touching both China and the Soviet Union.

North of the Hindu Kush, the semidesert plains of Turkistan stretch as far as the Amu Darya River. The western region of Afghanistan, around Herat, is an extension of the Iranian plateau. The southwest is an enormous, rocky desert. Hazarajat province sits at the heart of the central mountains. Finally, to the east, there are more mountains, reaching from Badakhshan in the north through Nuristan to Paktia province in the south.

In general the Afghan terrain is bare and much eroded. There are still forests in the region of Kunar and Nuristan, and also in Paktia province, but these too are steadily disappearing. Summers are hot and dry, winters harsh. Rain falls from December through February; and from November through March the mountains are covered with snow, making it difficult to travel through them. In the desert regions of the southwest, a wind called the "120 days" blows from July to September.

Almost all of rural Afghanistan is plagued by problems that result from the constant efforts to irrigate the arid land: as in many other Asian countries, the challenge is not to find water but to control it. In Afghanistan it is channeled from four major rivers and tributaries: the Amu Darya in the north; the Hari Rud in the west; the Kabul in the east; and the Helmand-Arghandab in the southwest and southeast, which provides water for more than two-thirds of the country. But much of Afghanistan is still without water, and barely 15 percent of the land is cultivated: a little more than 6 million hectares of the irrigated land, which is called *abi,* and 1.5 million hectares of the dry land known as *lalmi.* The most extensive cultivated regions are found north of the Hindu Kush, where cotton is grown.

Ethnically, the people of Afghanistan are primarily of two different physical types: Indo-Europeans of a Mediterranean sort (this includes the Pushtun, Tajik, Nuristani, and Baluchi peoples) and Turco-Mongolians (including the Hazara, Turkoman, Uzbek, Aimaq, and Khirgiz groups). A third group, the Dravidian Brahuis, account for a very small fraction of the population.

The largest ethnic group is Pushtun: 40 percent of the Afghan population speaks Pushtun, a language related to Persian. They are a tribal people, Sunni Muslims, and they live for the most part in the south of the country, although they have also colonized small regions in the north and are ethnically akin to a group of some 8.5 million people called Pathans who live across the border in Pakistan. The Tajiks of northeastern Afghanistan account for 25–30 percent of the total population and are related to a group living outside the country, across the border in the U.S.S.R.; they too are largely Sunnite, and they speak Dari—the Afghan Persian. The Hazaras are a Mongolian people, Shiite Muslims in religion, who live in the Hindu Kush: they number over a million and they speak Hazarigi, a language similar to Dari. The Uzbeks, living in the northern central region, are thought to include some million people; they speak a language similar to Turkish, and are Sunnites, too.

In the west of Hazarajat province, there are close to 800,000 Aimaqs, shephard nomads who speak Dari and worship as Sunnites. The Nuristani, the "kafirs," or infidels, until the last century, whose native province is a natural fortress in the east of the country, account for only 2 percent of the population but are extraordinarily distinct as a group, maintaining traditional religious rites as well as their own language. There are some 250,000 Turkomen who live in the northwestern steppes of Afghanistan across the border from a group of Soviet Turkomen. They speak a language related to Turkish and are Sunnite. Many of them came to Afghanistan during the 1920s, refugees from the U.S.S.R., where the government was suppressing Muslim freedom fighters (known as "Basmachis," or bandits).*

The Baluchis, who number close to 150,000, live in the southwestern desert region and speak a language related to Persian. They are Sunni nomads, akin to Baluchi peoples now found in Pakistan and Iran. The two smallest ethnic groups of Afghanistan are the Sunni Brahuis, who live among the Baluchis, and the several thousand Khirgiz, who have

---

* In toto, some 80 percent of the population are Sunni Muslims of the Hanafi sect, while only 20 percent are Shiite.

been displaced from the Wakhan Corridor, in the northwest corner of Afghanistan (for strategic reasons, the Corridor has in effect been annexed by the Soviet Union).*

The two principal languages of Afghanistan are Pushtun and Dari, a Persian court language still used largely by aristocratic families and in the town, particularly in Kabul.

Poetry, especially oral poetry, is extremely important in Afghan society. Much-admired troubadors sing either the epic cycles that are popular among Turkish-speaking Afghans or the warrior-poet tales that Pushtuns prefer. Khushal Khan Khattak—a tribal chief, a brave warrior, and a poet who sings about love as well as war†—is a traditional kind of hero, popular in tribal societies throughout the region that stretches from the Balkans through the Caucasus to the frontiers of the Indian world. He is a hero of steppes and mountains, of societies dominated by men with strict rules about how to live and how to die—societies where physical courage is still essential and even victory is accompanied by a reminder of mortality:

> *If glory is found in the jaws of a lion,*
> *Go tear it out of his mouth.*
> *You will have prestige and honors.*
> *If you fail, die like a man.*

Afghan folk tales hold that a coward killed in battle must not be buried according to traditional religious rites—which means that his spirit will never reach paradise.

---

* In the cities of Afghanistan there are also several thousand Hindus, Sikhs, and Kizilbachis, who are Shiite Muslims.

† D. Mackenzie, *Poems from the Divan of Khushal Khan Khattak* (London, 1963). For a less Victorian translation, see O. Carroe and E. Howell, *The Poems of Khushal Khan Khattak* (Peshawar, 1963).

Tribal Afghan societies are by nature isolated from the outside world, but their hostility and suspicion of outsiders are tempered by considerable hospitality. As in most traditional mountain societies, vendettas, known in Afghanistan as *badal,* are a classic means of avenging one's honor. It is assumed in these warring societies that men carry some sort of arms, whether daggers or guns, and Afghans take extraordinary care of their arms.

In this country without railroads, most people travel by bus or truck and, since the war began, by foot, on horseback, or even on the camels usually reserved as pack animals. Horses are used mainly in the north, where they are ridden in the dramatic traditional game of *buzkashi,* a "war game" that is the ancestor of polo.

Before the *coup d'état* of April 1978, Afghanistan was one of the most backward countries in the world. Outside of Kabul and a few cities like Herat and Kandahar, Afghan society is still wholly traditional, untouched even by colonial rule. Like northern Yemen before 1962, it has known none of the distortions and dislocations that skew both society and economy in most underdeveloped countries.

The decade between 1955 and 1965 brought some change to Afghanistan, the result of efforts and aid by both the United States and the Soviet Union. Bigger businesses began to emerge in Kabul, Herat, and Kandahar, and the growth of these cities spawned new social classes and strengthened others, such as employees in the state bureaucracy, that had previously been weak. Although migration from the countryside was relatively slight, it brought Hazaras and other peasants to the cities, where they found jobs as unskilled workers and common laborers in the building trades. A class of urban Tajik merchants also flourished.

Still, the country's industrial sector remained embryonic. At the time of the *coup d'état*, the industrial working class in Afghanistan included not more than 35,000 laborers, although some million Afghans had gone to Iran and the Persian Gulf in search of work in the oil fields.

The population of Afghanistan was generally estimated at from 14 to 19 million*—there may have been 15 million inhabitants by 1980. Infant mortality rates are extremely high—one out of every two Afghan children dies before it is five years old—and 90 to 95 percent of the population is illiterate.

The considerable obstacles that block development in Afghanistan are particularly evident in the towns. In Kabul, for example, there is much resentment of the aristocratic consumer class and the corrupt and inefficient government bureaucracy, which, by blocking the promotion of officials from the lower classes, makes social change virtually impossible. The frustration of these officials is often expressed ideologically, in radically modernist objection to liberal policies, as Marxism.

At the beginning of 1978, there were some 750,000 people living in Kabul. According to the only existing statistics concerning their income—statistics drawn from a survey poll taken in 1969—6 percent of the population spent 40 percent of all earnings, while 56 percent of the population spent less than 15 percent.

Of the 13 million people who live in the Afghan countryside, close to 2.5 million are nomads; they often have a considerable role in the lending of money among country people, as well as in commercial trading. As to rural land holdings,

---

* *UN Yearbook* (1975). In 1973, AID estimated as low as 12 million.

the only available statistics come from a survey of some 1.5 million families done in 1973. Of this group, close to 40 per-cent—about 500,000 families—were without land altogether; yet there are very few big landowners, and together they own no more than 8 percent of the land.

AREA (HECTARES)	PERCENTAGE OF ALL LANDOWNERS	PERCENTAGE OF LAND
0 – 0.5	40	4
0.6– 3.9	40	25
4 –19.9	17.8	29
20 –99.9	2	34
100 or more	0.2	8

Source: *The Area Handbook of Afghanistan* (Kabul, 1973), p. 36.

Considerably more land could be cultivated if the irriga-tion systems were improved, and there is room for expansion of animal farming, which is done mostly by nomad peoples. But despite this potential for growth, most Afghans still live in very backward conditions. According to official statistics, few people can expect to live beyond the age of thirty-five, while nearly half of the population suffers from epidemic dis-eases such as intestinal parasites—conveyed in the usually undrinkable water.

The authority of tribal headmen, or *khans,* goes for the most part unquestioned in rural Afghanistan, as does the power of the 250,000 religious leaders, or *mullahs,* who have for decades opposed any reforms that might threaten their in-fluence or undermine traditional customs. Thus, Afghan women still enjoy few rights, either in the law courts or at home, and even a family code passed in 1972 did not abolish polygamy.

Afghanistan is one of the twenty poorest countries in the world, but poverty has a different meaning in an underpopulated country where traditional social patterns are still largely intact, than in countries where inherited structures have been dislocated and destabilized. In 1967, there were some 14,205 rural villages in Afghanistan, and it was estimated that some 14 percent of the population lived in cities, another 14 percent were nomad or seminomad, and 72 percent were sedentary farmers.*

The arrangement of houses in an Afghan village is determined by two factors: the water supply and the village defense system. A typical house is made of bricks and dry earth, covered over by a kind of stucco made of straw mixed with mud. (Only in Nuristan is the pattern different: there, houses are built high, clinging to the sides of the mountains, and made of wood that is often elaborately carved.)

The survival of a typical Afghan farm depends on a successful combination of five basic components: land, water, seeds, work animals (or, in rare cases, farm machinery), and human labor. In general, the landowner controls land and water and also usually provides the farmer with whatever seeds he needs. Most landowners claim three-fifths of the harvest, although those who also provide pack animals claim up to four-fifths. The French scholar Olivier Roy† explains how this works:

"The land itself varies widely in different regions, but certain things are constant throughout the country. Large land holdings (over 100 hectares, hardly an enormous farm) are extremely rare. A rich peasant owns perhaps 10 hectares of irrigated land, a more modest peasant owns 2 to 4 hectares,

---

* Only a few cities claimed more than 100,000 inhabitants in 1976: Kabul (750,000), Kandahar (200,000), Herat (150,000), Kunduz (110,000). *The Area Handbook of Afghanistan* (Kabul, 1975).

† Olivier Roy, "Afghanistan: la 'révolution' par le vide," *Esprit*, May 1980, pp. 80–81.

and poor peasants own little or nothing. It is simply not true, as some reports from Afghanistan have claimed, that society there is divided into two classes: big landowners and landless peasants. My observations in the town of Alingar in Laghman province confirm Gilbert Étienne's figures*: half are modest landowners, largely self-sufficient farmers; and a quarter are peasants without land, who work as hired help on other people's farms, in most cases for a salary alone, without any share in the harvest or lasting connection with the land they work. These percentages vary slightly in the mountains and the northern plains, but overall most Afghan peasants are independent landowners with small holdings.

"But then, Afghan land has no value unless it is irrigated: land is less scarce than water is. Unirrigated land, called *lalmi,* is freehold: whoever cultivates it is entitled to the harvest. Only when there is water does it matter who owns the land—and only then do local notables jockey for power by building supplementary water towers. This is not to say that Afghan society is egalitarian or democratic. Certainly local headmen, called *arbab* or *mälek,* exploit less powerful and poorer peasants; but their relations cannot be characterized as feudal.

"Sometimes the exploitation is fairly crude: the landowner hires an agricultural worker or leases the land to a sharecropper, who keeps between one-sixth and one-half of the harvest, depending on whether he brings his own tools and seeds. A more subtle form of exploitation is the system known as *gerao:* a peasant borrows money at the exorbitant lending rate of 50 percent and gives whatever he harvests to his creditor to pay off the debt—which of course doubles regularly thanks to the interest rate. Certainly being in debt is a part of an Af-

---

* In his report ''L'Afghanistan ou les aléas de la coopération'' (Paris, 1972).

ghan peasant's life: scraping by between two harvests, or at the time of a daughter's marriage, when the dowry expected can be as high as $2000.

"But this is hardly class exploitation: the small landowner burdened by debts still lives like a small landowner, especially if his creditor is another small landowner rather than a local notable. And in the end, the problem of exploitation fades before the fundamental problem of demographic pressure. Within each family, a peasant's plot of land becomes smaller with every generation: there is little migration to the city, and the yield of the farm does not increase. Before the Marxists came to power in the late 1970s, many peasant families were getting poorer every year; but even the land reform, carried out much against the wills of the peasants by the new Marxist regime, was not enough to stem this steady erosion.

"In the end the only solution will be to increase the country's arable land by improving irrigation. This is what many Afghans expected would come with the installation of a new regime. They also hoped that the new government would reform the *gerao* mortgage system and ensure a fairer distribution of water and fertilizer. They did not expect that their traditional society would be thrown into disorder. Certainly the new socialist regime installed in April 1978 was not brought to power by a revolutionary crisis in the countryside: traditional peasant society was well ordered and flexible.

"For a European Marxist, the word 'feudal' has less to do with what Marx called a mode of production than with a state of technical retardation; it is a word that one applies to the entire civilization of a country. Thus a country's backwardness is used today, just as it was by nineteenth-century colonialists, to justify intervention in its internal affairs. European

Marxist arguments used to justify the Soviet intervention in Afghanistan show the same scorn for the culture of a country with weak technology, the same blind faith in progress that has nothing to do with what is left of the past—the same ethnocentrism.

"The only thing that Marx would call 'feudal' about rural society in Afghanistan is its total disregard for the state. There are no guaranteed civil rights; no official land surveys; no local government administration except in the cities. The *mälek* of each village represents his townspeople to the central government in disputes about taxes or military recruitment. As local headman, he also takes charge of paying the *mullah,* welcoming outside visitors, and sometimes, particularly in Nuristan, financing local public works.

"The new socialist regime is represented in the countryside by a handful of school teachers and, more rarely, by a small garrison: some dozen soldiers dressed in ragged uniforms— before the Soviets dressed them—who while away the time in a decrepit fortress commanded by a district chief called a *hakim.* From time to time a Land-Rover full of officials passes through on an inspection tour. But most Afghans try to have as little as possible to do with the central government: even before the Marxist revolution they knew that it brought only worries—and the revolution hardly persuaded them otherwise. The state is Kabul, and most Afghan country people see Kabul as the source of all that is corrupt and sinful and impious.

"Culturally and in his daily routines, the Afghan peasant is closer to the local headman than to any government official or revolutionary leader—men who come from the city wearing Western clothes and are clearly bored by the peasants' problems. Besides, the local headman is nothing like a European country squire: peasants and headmen dress alike and speak with identical accents; they see each other every day; their sons are educated by the same *mullah*. It is difficult for Westerners to look behind the polite codes of an Afghan village and to grasp what it is that marks the difference between a headman and an ordinary peasant. In the end, their social cohesion derives in large part from their religion."

The history of modern Afghanistan's relations with the Soviet Union begins shortly after the Bolshevik Revolution. Britain retained control of Afghanistan's foreign policy until the end of World War I, but when the country began to manage its own affairs in 1919, it quickly signed treaties with several nations, including France. Its first treaty with Russia dates from 1921, only a few years after the Revolution. A second followed in 1926: a Treaty of Neutrality and Nonaggression that established air routes between Tashkent and Kabul. In 1934, Afghanistan became a member of the League of Nations; and in 1936, it signed a pact of friendship with the United States. But on the eve of World War II, Germany was the foreign power with most influence in Afghanistan, and Kabul remained neutral throughout the war.

After the war, when the British withdrew from the Indian subcontinent, and India and Pakistan were formed, the question of the disposition of Pushtunistan first came to international attention. The "Pathans" of the North-West Frontier Province had for decades been resisting British rule, and it was hardly surprising that the new Afghan state, with its own large Pushtun population, should support their demands for self-determination.

In 1950, the U.S.S.R. and Afghanistan signed an economic agreement: the Soviet Union would provide sugar, cotton, and oil in exchange for wool and raw cotton. By 1952, trade between the two countries had doubled, accounting for some 20 percent of Afghan exports. In December 1955, Khrushchev and Bulganin stopped in Kabul on their way home from India; this visit was followed by a million-dollar development loan and a ten-year extension of the old Soviet-Afghan Treaty of Neutrality and Nonaggression. Soon a series of joint projects was under way: an airport for Kabul and a road through the Salang Pass from the Soviet border to Kabul—the road used by Soviet tanks in 1979.

The United States also helped to push Afghanistan toward the Soviet Union—by supporting its rival, Pakistan, on the issue of Pushtunistan, and refusing in 1954–55 to sell it arms. It was at that time that officers from the Afghan army were first sent to be trained in the U.S.S.R., and Soviet advisers worked out Afghanistan's first five-year economic plan for the period from 1956 to 1961.

In 1961, tensions with Pakistan were strained concerning the question of Pushtunistan, and Afghanistan turned to the Soviet Union for help. Khrushchev offered only moral support, while Pakistan joined the United States both in the CENTO pact with Turkey and Iran, and in the Southeast Asia Treaty Organization (SEATO).

Soviet economic aid continued to pour into Afghanistan. Between 1955 and 1965, Kabul received some $552 million from Moscow (compared to some $350 million from the United States). After 1965, American aid shrank even more, amounting to only $150 million per annum during the years 1965 to 1977, while the Soviet figure rose to $750 million.

By the time King Mohammad Zahir came to power in 1964, the Soviet Union had made sure that it had considerable influence inside Afghanistan, largely by means of its advisers serving in key government ministries. But there was little these Russians could do to save the government of King

Zahir, a corrupt and autocratic constitutional monarchy, which banned all political parties and soon accumulated a sizable foreign debt. Zahir allowed the economy to become excessively dependent on foreign aid, and undertook virtually no internal social or economic reforms. Two-thirds of the country's industry belonged to the state, and functioned at only about 50 percent capacity. The peasants continued to see to their own needs as best they could until in 1971 a severe drought led to famine. Zahir's liberal constitution remained a dead letter; the promise of political liberty was never kept; power was confiscated by dynasty and court. In 1973, the king was overthrown by his cousin Mohammad Daud Khan, who proclaimed a republic.

Economic affairs improved markedly during the five years of Daud's republic. Afghanistan's balance of payments surplus rose from $2.2 million in 1973 to some $65 million in 1977, while currency reserves jumped from $18 million to $128 million during the period 1972–78. Both the quality and quantity of exports climbed, and wages flowed back into the country from the Afghans who had gone to work in the oil fields of the Persian Gulf. But the recovery also depended in large part on increasing foreign aid; and the economy remained fragile and uncertain, burdened by accumulating debt.

Daud's political record was less impressive. He came to power with the help of a number of ministers from the Marxist-Leninist Parcham faction, but as soon as he was confidently installed, leftists were purged from the administration. Meanwhile, a fundamentalist opposition, led by the Islamic Party, was growing steadily across the border in Pakistan, where it received considerable financial support. This group won a significant following among discontented peasants, but a rebellion launched in July 1975 from Panchir was quickly suppressed by the Afghan army.

In foreign affairs, Daud relied more and more on support from Iran and Saudi Arabia, while at home power remained in the hands of the old aristocratic classes. Promised modernization did not take place. Politics remained a game of patronage and family influence; and as always before, Afghan peasants took no part in governing the country.

"For the most part, government functionaries were no more privileged than other deprived groups. But as soon as one rose above a certain level in the hierarchy of state power, anything could be bought. Personal fortunes were made at the expense of the population, monies collected in one guise or another. The incompetent administration grew, feeding on feudal corruption, until size alone would have made it inefficient. Instead of functioning as a modern state, the Afghan bureaucracy helped only to block the country's development.

"A middle class began to emerge, petty officials in the rapidly growing government or people who had taken advantage of the first economic development made possible by foreign aid. But they soon found that they could not rise above the status of petty bourgeoisie, blocked as they were by the very presence of a grasping aristocratic class. It was only a matter of time before the middle classes became frustrated and angry with this arrangement, its rigidity and intrinsic inefficiency. Problems were only aggravated by the administrative mismanagement of the economy."*

Thus neither the monarchy nor Daud's republican government was able to bring the country to the point of

---

* Pierre Gentelle, "Non-développement et sous-développement," *Temps modernes*, special issue on Afghanistan, July-August 1980, Nos. 408–9.

"take-off"—to the beginning of sustained and autonomous economic growth. The impatience of the new elite classes educated abroad—particularly the officers trained in the Soviet Union—steadily grew.

AFGHAN EXPORTS (1975–76)

	VALUE (in millions of dollars)	PERCENTAGE OF TOTAL
dried fruit	54.7	23.2
natural gas	46.3	19.6
cotton	35.3	15.0
fresh fruit	20.1	8.6
rugs	16.1	6.8
caracul sheepskin	10.4	4.4
miscellaneous	6.6	2.7

In 1975–76, imports were 30 percent greater than exports.
Source: Ministry of Planning

PRINCIPAL TRADING PARTNERS
(in millions of dollars)

IMPORTS		EXPORTS	
U.S.S.R.	83.4	U.S.S.R.	86.4
Japan	67.6	Pakistan	29.0
West Germany	43.5	India	26.0
India	41.4	West Germany	22.3
U.S.	22.8	U.K.	15.1

In 1975, 41 percent of Afghanistan's exports went to socialist countries.
Source: *The Middle East and North Africa 1979–80* (London, 1980).

3 FROM THE COUP D'ÉTAT TO THE SOVIET INVASION

Like much that happens in Afghanistan, the emergence of the left came very late, even in comparison to the rest of Central Asia. The first democratic movement did not appear until sometime after World War II, when an organization called Awakened Youth was founded in Kabul in 1949. It survived for a few years in a relatively liberal climate before being banned in 1952. Another significant leftist group appeared in 1965, when the Democratic Party of the People of Afghanistan (Jamiyati demokratiki i Khalq i Afghanistan) held its first congress in Kabul. At the time, the party's central committee included, among others, Nur Mohammad Taraki and Babrak Karmal, a student leader from the University of Kabul.

The DPPA grew considerably between 1967 and 1970, as good government jobs became rare, a scarcity that increased unrest among Afghan students. Until the early 1960s, a typical son of a good family had passed almost automatically from university to a job in the government bureaucracy. But as most of the better jobs were now filled, and it became more

31

difficult to advance from the lower ranks of the administration, many high school students found it impossible even to enter university. Some were able to get modest jobs; others found no work at all.

The DPPA won two parliamentary seats in the election of 1969: one went to Babrak Karmal, the other to Hafizullah Amin, an ambitious young party leader who had studied in the United States and worked in the Afghan embassy in Washington as well as in the American embassy in Kabul. But the party was already split in an internal schism, dating from 1967, between Babrak Karmal's Parcham faction and the Khalq faction led by Amin and Taraki. Perhaps the most marked difference between the two groups (which both took their names from party newspapers) was in the social classes from which they drew their followers. Parcham members came from a more established milieu and were generally people who had been urban-dwellers for some generations, while Khalq followers came for the most part from modest provincial families.

This meant linguistic differences as well as cultural ones, for although the Afghan state was founded by Pushtuns, the aristocracy had traditionally disdained Pushtun culture and adopted Dari as its language. The Pushtuns who came to live in the cities learned Dari, a sign of sophistication. Thus most Parchami are Persian-speakers, although they are Pushtun in origin. But Khalqi, who have been urban-dwellers for rarely more than one generation, continue to speak Pushtun with some pride: for them, it is a symbol of ethnic identity.

As for doctrine, Parcham supports a democratic revolution, national in scope and ideology but not necessarily socialist, at least not at the beginning. Its leader, Babrak Karmal, is the son of a high-ranking army officer and was himself a member of parliament. He believes that his followers should embrace whatever alliances offer themselves in the interest of the revolution, and in 1973 Parcham collaborated with Daud in overthrowing the monarchy—until Daud excluded them from power. The Khalq faction, on the other hand, opposes broad alliances and refused to collaborate with Daud.

In the early 1970s, the Khalq leader Hafizullah Amin began to build a clandestine base of support among army officers, and by the time the Khalq and Parcham factions joined in loose coalition again, in July 1977, Amin was at the top of the hierarchy. Still, relations between the two factions were rarely harmonious. Khalq accused Parcham of collaborating with the republican government determined to destroy them, while Parcham accused Hafizullah Amin of working for the CIA.

After 1975, the Daud regime did in fact dismiss its Parcham ministers, as it opted for a more and more active collaboration with the Shah of Iran. Encouraged by the Shah to reduce Afghan dependence on the Soviet Union, Daud made an effort to improve the country's relations with Pakistan, largely by muting Afghan claims about Pushtunistan. Before long, he was also receiving considerable financial aid from the Shah of Iran and was able to cut some economic ties to Moscow.

Daud also faced internal opposition from several small movements to the left of the DDPA. One small group, called the National Oppression Party (Settam-e-Melli), was a Maoist (and Shiite) splinter of the DPPA, based in large part in the Tajik regions of Badakhshan and opposed above all to the creation of a greater Pushtunistan. Another group, called Eternal Flame (Shula-e-Jawid), claimed to be "Marxist-Leninist" and denounced the "revisionism" of the DPPA; it too opposed a greater Pushtunistan and rejected Pushtun domination of Afghan society.

In November 1977, Daud formed a new cabinet controlled

by extreme conservatives. The leftist opposition grew increasingly restless and a crisis seemed imminent. In early spring 1978, on the eve of the *coup d'état,* Daud announced a series of reforms and arrested a considerable part of the Afghan left.

On April 17, 1978, Mir Akbar Khyber, the editor of the Parcham newspaper, was assassinated in Kabul. He was a well-known figure, a member of the central committee of the DPPA, and his funeral was the occasion of a large anti-government demonstration that ended on the steps of the American embassy. On April 26, President Daud had some half-dozen DPPA leaders arrested, including Nur Mohammad Taraki, Babrak Karmal, and Hafizullah Amin. By chance, Amin was arrested somewhat after the other leaders, and before going into custody he advised a group of army officers to take action against the regime. A group from the Fifteenth Brigade, stationed some kilometers from the capital, arrived in Kabul the next morning in a column of tanks, seizing the airport and the palace. This *coup d'état* met with no resistance except from the garrison of Jalalabad. Daud and his family were immediately killed.

In their first official declaration, the new leaders of what was now called the Democratic Republic of Afghanistan proclaimed their nationalism and their respect for Islam. They also pledged the regime to economic and social justice, and declared their respect for all treaties previously signed by Afghanistan, confirming that as before the country would be nonaligned. Still, the new government did not hide its intention to transform Afghan society at the expense of its traditionally privileged classes.

On April 30, it was declared that the presidency of the republic would go to Nur Mohammad Taraki, who was already, as secretary-general of the DPPA, functioning as the prime minister. The next day, a revolutionary council was established: its thirty civilian and five military members then elected a cabinet of twenty-one, including three army officers and a number of nationalists. The Khalq faction continued to control the ruling coalition, but the vice-presidency was given to Babrak Karmal, secretary-general of Parcham.

At first, this new Afghan government was fairly popular: most Afghans had been disappointed by Daud's corrupt regime, which had failed to bring about much-promised agrarian reforms or a more democratic state. Support for the new regime was strongest in Kabul, where there were open demonstrations, but even the countryside seemed sympathetic, refusing for the most part to participate in the armed resistance groups that were launched by fundamentalist movements that had been operating across the border in Pakistan since 1973.

On May 9, the new government announced its program: a "national democratic" platform, opposed to "feudalism," calling on workers, peasants, artisans, and the intelligentsia to unite in support of the DPPA. The government recognized the cultural rights of all ethnic and national minorities. It banned forced marriages and ruled that no girls be wed before the age of sixteen. The poorest peasants found that their debts were canceled by Decree 6, a measure confirmed two months later, which abolished all peasants' debts as well as usury. The new regime also promised that agrarian reforms would be implemented after two years of preliminary study. The regime avoided the Marxist-Leninist label but its intentions were clear enough.* At that time, there were some 3000 Soviet advisers in Afghanistan.

But the coalition government lasted hardly three months. Soon Parcham members, nationalists, and leaders of ethnic

---

* The excellent observer of African and Asian politics Fred Halliday was not taken in. See the *New Left Review,* November–December 1978, No. 112.

minorities who had helped to bring the new regime to power were pushed out of the government. Babrak Karmal was made ambassador to Prague, thus cutting short his efforts to bring into the government more nationalist leaders like Major General Abdul Qadar—minister of defense and one of the chief strategists behind the coup. Nur Ahmad, former minister of the interior, was sent to Washington, and Anahita Rabtezad was packed off to Belgrade. Meanwhile, several important army units promised to support the Khalq faction. In August, a number of nationalists were arrested and accused of conspiring against the government; among them were Major General Abdul Qadar; the chief of staff, Shahpur Ahmadzai; and several other members of the cabinet—all of them more or less protégés of the Parcham faction. Two months later, the prisoners were forced to confess their allegiance to Parcham, and a number of other leading members of that group were expelled from the government by the Revolutionary Council. The regime also recalled the Parcham leaders who had been sent abroad; not surprisingly, they refused to return.

By September, the Khalq faction had taken firm control of Afghanistan, and it launched a series of further reforms designed to win support from the masses. Decree 7, issued in October, gave full legal rights to women, banning forced marriages and dowries. Decree 8 set guidelines for agrarian reform, restricting each peasant's holdings to thirty *jerib* (six hectares) of fertile land and 300 *jerib* (sixty hectares) of unirrigated land. This reform ignored the enormous variety of existing Afghan rules for land ownership and cultivation and also the cultural patterns based on these rules in different tribes and regions of the country. For Khalq leaders, social relations in rural Afghanistan were best described by the

Marxist term "feudal": one phase in the series that runs from primitive community, through enslavement, feudalism, and capitalism to socialism. In thinking this way, the Khalqi also ignored the complexity of Afghan farming, a system whose provision of irrigation, seeds, work animals, and manual labor is as important as the ownership of land. By interfering with that one element, Khalq leaders upset the delicate equilibrium of the entire society.

Thus blinded to the importance of traditional social patterns, the dogmatic Khalq leaders soon found that it was impossible to isolate large landowners from the rest of peasant society, that most peasants had little political experience to guide them in expropriating the land of village headmen, and that the 130,000 families who did in fact benefit from Khalq reforms were unable to protect themselves when the former owners began to reclaim the lands. It was futile in any case to redistribute the land to the peasants without allowing them to control both irrigation and the distribution of seeds. As it turned out, many peasants returned their new land to its previous owners in exchange for seeds and water.*

The leaders of the Khalq regime had made no preliminary investigations of ownership patterns; they had neither survey information nor local leaders with knowledge of actual conditions in the countryside. In short, it would have been virtually impossible for them to devise a successful land-reform program. As it was, their reforms were implemented by blundering and often brutal officials from the city who dropped into the countryside by parachute. And in many cases, the Khalq regime's attempted reforms succeeded only in unifying villagers and even entire tribes around local leaders opposed

---

* See Olivier Roy, "Afghanistan: la révolution par le vide," *Esprit*, May 1980.

to the central authority of the state. What they resented most was the outsiders' intervention in tribal and regional affairs where they were used to governing autonomously.

The Khalq regime's rural literacy campaign was also conceived in the name of progress and implemented without concern for local political consequences: state officials would arrive in a village, assemble the entire population, and divide it into classes to learn reading and writing. The next day, most of the villagers would not show up, mainly because they thought women should not appear in public. The Khalq leaders dismissed this as a backward attitude, and tried using force to assemble both men and women. In some cases the townspeople merely sent them packing; in other villages, they were assassinated.* Khalq leaders persisted in trying to implement these and other reforms, generally accompanied by repressive measures, throughout the winter of 1978. By the end of the winter, pockets of rebellion and resistance had developed in Nuristan, Kunar, and Paktia provinces.

In the cities, the rupture between Khalq and Parcham factions brought renewed and ever stronger repression. Price controls were instituted, spreading discontent among the merchant classes. In November, a team of Soviet advisers arrived in Kabul to prepare a new seven-year plan, intended to replace the 1976–83 plan which had been effectively annulled by the fall of President Daud.

On December 5, Nur Mohammad Taraki went to Moscow to sign a twenty-year Treaty of Friendship and Cooperation between Russia and Afghanistan. Some eight weeks later, on February 14, 1979, the American ambassador in Kabul, Adolph Dubs, was kidnapped by members of the National Oppression Party, the small group of Maoist and Shiite mili-

---

* Casterac and Levant, in *Le Monde diplomatique,* February 1980.

tants. Both the ambassador and his kidnappers were killed by Afghan security forces who attempted to rescue the American official.

Little by little insurrection spread spontaneously throughout Afghanistan during February, March, and April: by midspring it had touched most of the twenty-nine provinces. Antigovernment feeling was strongest in provinces such as Hazarajat, Nuristan, and Badakhshan, where religious and geographical isolation reinforced people's desire for regional autonomy.

On March 24, a garrison of soldiers in Herat rose up against a group of Soviet advisers who had ordered Afghan troops to fire on antigovernment demonstrators. The advisers and their families were killed. Several days later Nur Mohammad Taraki, who had for some time been serving as president and prime minister, ceded the second post to Hafizullah Amin, who was by now clearly the strong man of the regime. Both Amin and Taraki were among the nine members of the Homeland High Defense Council, which met for the first time on April 2. On April 6, a Soviet delegation headed by General Alexei Yepichev, president for political affairs of the Soviet army and navy, arrived in Kabul. When Yepichev left, his compatriot Vassili Safrontchuk was given the job of coordinating Soviet policy in Afghanistan—an official post that came with an office in the government building right next to Taraki's own suite. By that time there were some 5000 Soviet advisers in Afghanistan.

The uprising in Herat marked a significant change in climate throughout the country. After April the regime was no longer merely isolated from peasants in the countryside, but divided by open hostility from an overwhelming majority of all the people. The regime had no choice now but to crush much of the population. Hafizullah Amin's secret police and a repressive civilian police force went into action across Afghanistan, and army troops were sent into the countryside to subdue "feudal" villagers. But the Homeland High Defense Council feared defections in the ranks, and soon it confined its soldiers to barracks. They were replaced by planes and MI-24 helicopters, which began systematic bombing of rebellious tribal villages. By December 1979, UN officials estimate, some 400,000 refugees from Afghanistan's rural villages had crossed the border to Pakistan. Members of insurgent tribes remaining in Kabul were placed in preventive detention, as was anyone suspected of opposing the regime. On June 23, a commando from the Hazara tribe attacked a military police station in Kabul. Violence and repression intensified.

On July 27, Hafizullah Amin became secretary of the party central committee and minister of defense. He kept the title of prime minister and continued to oversee the security police. In effect, he now entirely controlled the apparatus of the state. Amin, himself very much a product of traditional Afghan society, was a man more rigid in personality than either Taraki or Babrak Karmal, and he was also greatly embittered by political developments since the coup, for which he had been primarily responsible: although obviously the strong man of the regime, he was only now being officially acknowledged as its principal leader.

The DPPA announced during August that some 325,000 hectares of land had been distributed to 132,000 families. Nothing was said about the number of Khalq officials who had disappeared trying to implement this reform. In July, entire units of the Afghan army either deserted or joined the rebel forces, and by late 1979 the regular army had been reduced to close to half of its earlier 85,000 men. On August 5, a mutiny occurred at the Bala Hissar garrison near Kabul, a unit made up largely of Khalq officers. Several officers were arrested and the garrison was eventually subdued, but not without tanks and fighting planes. A second mutiny took place on August 12, in Kandahar.

By this time, the MIG-21 planes used to put down local uprisings were manned, more often than not, by Soviet pilots. Then in September, Soviet troops took charge of an important air force base at Bagram, some miles north of Kabul. The crisis had become acute. The government was wholly isolated from the Afghan people—rebellious villagers as well as people from more educated classes in the towns, who were appalled by the regime's repressive tactics. Mass arrests were commonly followed by torture and execution without trial. Police terror was common in the city as well as the countryside, where virtually all social groups joined in the rebellion. Ethnic groups, religious movements, tribal factions, regional groups, radical leftist factions like Settam-e-Melli and Shula-e-Jawid—some rejected the regime for religious reasons, others because they resented its centralized authority. The rebellion was diverse and wholly uncoordinated, raising spontaneously among the people.

By early autumn, the regime recognized that something must be done: its repressive measures were not going to contain the revolt. On September 10, President Taraki stopped in Moscow on his way home from a conference of nonaligned countries in Havana. He met with Leonid Brezhnev and together they decided that Kabul should return to a program of democratic nationalism, inviting Parcham to rejoin the government and freeing all political prisoners. In effect, this decision meant that Hafizullah Amin would have to be exiled or killed, since he controlled the machinery of the wholly Khalq regime.

Amin learned of the Moscow meeting, and the danger

threatening him, from one of his agents who was posing as Taraki's *aide de camp*. On September 14, Amin was summoned to the presidential palace, but instead his own men arrested Taraki, who, several weeks later, was executed.

On September 16, Amin added the presidency of the Homeland High Defense Council to his list of posts. Taking over as head of state, he knew that the regime was still dependent on the Soviet Union for both economic and military support; but as a nationalist, he refused to recognize the consequences of this dependence (a dependence that became more acute when the Shah of Iran fell and the new revolutionary government in Teheran expelled some thousands of immigrant Afghan workers, whose wages in the oil fields had been an important part of the economy of Afghanistan). On October 6, his government demanded that Russia recall its ambassador, while the minister of foreign affairs went before a meeting of socialist leaders and accused the Soviet ambassador of plotting to overthrow the regime in Kabul. A month later this ambassador was replaced, but not before Khalq leaders circulated documents accusing the Russians of having conspired with Taraki and his followers to provoke the crisis in September. In the meantime, several of Taraki's supporters fled to the Soviet Union.

Hafizullah Amin spent the months from October to December trying to enlarge his base of support. He wooed religious factions by promising to protect their cults. He shrewdly criticized Taraki for assuming too much personal power, and dissolved his own secret police—only to replace it some weeks later with another security force, called the Workers' Intelligence Organization and headed by one of his nephews. Then he announced that a commission would soon produce a new constitution, ending the regime's government by decree. He promised to protect small landowners and solicited support from several tribal chiefs. He also released a number of political prisoners.

But Amin still had very little room in which to maneuver: too much blood had been shed for tribal people to pardon him or his repressive regime. In any case, his apparently liberal reforms were accompanied by a far-reaching military counteroffensive against rebels in Kunar and Paktia provinces, an attack that drove several hundred thousand refugees from Kunar across the border into Pakistan. He also pressed the Pakistanis to close rebel strongholds across the border and cut lines of support leading into Afghanistan. Furthermore, the elections he promised did not take place.

The Soviet Union continued its efforts to influence the regime: S. Papurtin, the Soviet director of international security affairs, visited Kabul, followed by a team of Soviet advisers who tried to reorganize the Afghan secret police. Amin refused to allow them to do so, and tension between the two countries grew.

On December 27 Soviet troops intervened. Armored units made up in large part of Tajiks, Uzbeks, and Turkomen quickly surrounded Kabul and there were skirmishes outside of several government buildings. Amin was overthrown and immediately executed, along with several members of his family. Babrak Karmal was proclaimed president and prime minister, and a new government was announced that included Parcham leaders like Anahita Rabtezad, whom the Khalqi had pushed out of the government; others like Major General Abdul Qadar, who had been imprisoned; and also some of those who had fled to Russia after Taraki was executed.

Very quickly, as Babrak Karmal had immediately promised, close to 2000 political prisoners were freed.* "Rebels" were offered unconditional amnesty, and the new chief of state announced that it was time to reunite the country by political rather than military means. The regime began to give special attention to Islamic supporters, and "national democracy" replaced "workers' state" as the official description of the revolution.

In retrospect, it seems unlikely that the Khalq regime could have done other than fail in Afghanistan, given the nature of the movement and its tactics. There probably were no more than 4000 to 5000 militant members of the faction, most of them people from modest, country backgrounds. They had come to Afghanistan's towns and capital only recently, and often their education had been poor: the public schools like the Khushal Khan Khattak high school, which many of them had attended, were inferior to the French Istiqlal high school or the German Nedjat school—institutions that somewhat better-off families frequented. Their political education was rudimentary—often no more than casual reading of Soviet propaganda brochures. Once in power, they practiced what is sometimes called "underdeveloped Stalinism."

Afghan political power has traditionally been restricted to a small social group: the royal family, educated city people, and the rural aristocracy. Most Khalq officials were teachers or white-collar workers, people with intellectual aspirations who were poorly paid and lacked prestige: they were dissatisfied with their own status and also, more generally, with con-

---

* In November 1979, when Amin replaced Taraki as head of state, he announced that some 12,000 political prisoners had been executed by his predecessor. At the time there were probably close to 20,000 more political offenders incarcerated in Kabul. Karmal's decree obviously did not cover all of these.

ditions in their country. But for the most part they knew nothing of village life or tribal society. Optimistic volunteers, they believed they would be followed enthusiastically as soon as they announced a revolutionary program. They were surprised by the scorn and rejection of the peasants they thought they were helping, deeply shocked when villagers began to assassinate the officials sent out to implement the reforms. And they reacted with extreme brutality: repressive measures were directed against entire villages and even tribes. Moreover, once they were in power, party bureaucrats from modest social backgrounds were quick to expropriate luxurious dwellings. Within the party, corruption was commonplace, as was nepotism.

The rebellion against the Khalq faction began in the towns, a reaction to purges and indiscriminate imprisonment of political opponents, but it spread quickly to the countryside. And although Khalq officials found the peasants backward, they themselves were often extremely traditional: for the most part their modern ideology masked much simpler ethnic or regional rivalries. In many cases their Manichean beliefs derived from grudges based on family feuds or linguistic differences. (Thus, as a member of the Gilsaï branch of the Pushtun group, President Taraki often favored the Kalat-Kandahar region.) They tolerated no opposition within the government, just as Hafizullah Amin tolerated no opposition within the party. But factional fighting among Khalq leaders much weakened and isolated the movement. Taraki was the intellectual of the regime: a well-known novelist who headed the movement without dominating it. In contrast, Amin was a pragmatic organization man: the figure behind the *coup d'état,* in charge of the secret police, he ensured his control of the party early on by blocking an alliance between Taraki and Babrak Karmal.

The reforms undertaken by the new regime were, for the most part, necessary for the modernization of Afghanistan: elimination of peasant debts and usury, land reform, an attempt to change family patterns, a literacy campaign. But the Khalq's political tactics depended on the limited and often mechanical enthusiasm of its volunteers, a kind of sterile revolutionary fervor. In this, the Khalqi were not unlike the Khmer Rouge—in its intellectual poverty, political naïveté, and repressive brutality.

Another explanation for the failure of the Khalq regime lies in the nature of Afghan society, a deeply traditional world of tribal ways and village habits that had never been disturbed by colonial rulers. The Khalq regime hoped to bring into the modern industrial world a country where 85 percent of the population still lived on the land. They tried to teach peasants guided by tribal hierarchies and religious leaders to perceive society as an arrangement of antagonistic social classes. They failed to take account of the deep conservatism of most Afghans outside of Kabul—the only place where modern habits and modernist views had even a foothold. And they tried to impose centralized rule of law on a society where political differences were traditional. Of course, most members of the Khalq faction also themselves belonged to traditional Afghanistan society—a society used to deference to unquestioned authority and to the brutality of political groups who claim that they alone know what is good for the rest of the people. The desire to dominate without sharing power and a Manichean intolerance of any opposition are characteristic of traditional society and of avant-garde political groups. It was hardly surprising that the Khalq faction soon found itself not only isolated by factional struggle but undone by its own lack of flexibility in executing its policies.

4 THE AFGHAN RESISTANCE

A visit with the rebels in Afghanistan suggests two broad conclusions about the resistance there. The first is that it is an extremely popular movement that has arisen spontaneously among many different kinds of people with varying motives. It is not manpower that the guerrillas lack, but weapons. The second is that in its leadership organization, coordination, and strategy, the Afghan movement is one of the weakest liberation struggles in the world today.

In most other national liberation movements and armed struggles in the Third World—in Vietnam, Cuba, Algeria, Guinea-Bissau, and elsewhere—the principal task of the revolutionary vanguard was to win the support of at least part of the population, slowly, patiently building an underground political organization. In Afghanistan the pattern is different: during the winter of 1978–79, the Afghans joined in a spontaneous uprising against the Khalq government that had replaced Daud's republic; the resistance grew steadily, although in a fragmented and uncoordinated way, strongest first in

Nuristan and Hazarajat but soon spreading into Tajik and Pushtun regions. Even greater numbers joined the fight against the Soviet army and the Parcham regime it brought to power at the end of December 1979.

Insurrection began in late 1978 in Nuristan, a region known for its unusual customs and fierce independence; but it soon spread, first into Hazarajat and the Tajik regions north of the Hindu Kush and then, in the early spring of 1979, into the province of Herat. Only then did the Pushtun people begain to join the rebellion, particularly in Paktia province. Although the rebels' motives varied widely and the movement lacked a clear, common goal, they were united in their rejection of the regime: opposition among both landowners and landless peasants to its agrarian reform; a dislike of centralization and government interference in local affairs; a desire to protect traditional customs and religious values. New regions were drawn into the struggle as they came under pressure to cooperate with the government reforms; and rebels from extremely varied groups were united in a traditionalist, religious rejection of the Khalqi's atheism and their "communist" program. The rebellion remained entirely spontaneous, without coordinated leadership of any kind, for many months. Not until March 1979, when the government suppressed uprisings in Herat and bombed rebel camps in Ghazni, Kandahar, and Gardez, did the political parties based across the Pakistani border in Peshawar begin to win supporters in the countryside. The rebellion continued to spread during the spring, touching all regions of the country; many Afghan soldiers deserted to join the resistance; and by the end of the summer it was clear that the regime could not last much longer.

Today, the resistance movement controls most of the countryside of Afghanistan, in broad daylight as well as at night.

The government and its Soviet military support hold the towns and the main roads through the northwest plains and the semidesert region of the southwest, as well as a string of fortresses along the Pakistani border. The rebels are mainly peasants, and their local leaders are generally tribal chiefs or religious headmen. A generation of young leaders is slowly emerging.

Unlike virtually all guerrilla movements of Asia, Africa, or Latin America, the Afghan resistance has nothing new to show the visiting observer: no new elected village committee, for example; no program for the integration of women into the struggle; no new clinics or schools; no newly created stores that sell or exchange essential goods; no small workshops contributing to economic self-sufficiency of the sort one finds in guerrilla camps elsewhere throughout the world. The Afghan rebels have undertaken no political experiments or social improvements. In this respect, they resemble the Basmachi insurrectionists—the Muslims of the Bukhara emirate, now within the Soviet Union, who resisted the Bolshevik takeover and the reforms that followed during the 1920s.* Indeed, some of the tribesmen in northern Afghanistan are sons and grandsons of Basmachi peasants and nomads who fled across the border in the 1920s and 1930s, and they are traditionally anticommunist as well as anti-Soviet. The current Afghan resistance movement looks more like a traditional revolt of this kind than like modern guerrilla warfare. Among contemporary guerrilla movements only the Kenyan Mau Mau are less sophisticated in their strategy and organization.

---

* The Basmachis came from the Uzbek, Turkoman, and Tajik tribes, and they continued to harass the Red Army until 1928. When the Turkistan region fell to the Bolsheviks in 1922–23, Muslim leaders and Marxists like Sultan Galiev were purged. In 1924, the autonomous republics of Central Asia were conquered and replaced by the Soviet Socialist Republics, Uzbekistan, and Turkmenia, and Kirghiz and Kazakhstan in 1936. The emirate of Bukhara was divided between the republics of Uzbekistan and Tajilistan.

No group within the Afghan resistance, whether inside or outside the country, has a strategy or organizational plan that could unite the diverse rebel movement. Although certain individual fighters are well informed, few faction leaders have any significant knowledge about the enemy or about opportunities for foreign support. None of the Afghan rebel groups seems to recognize that no guerrilla struggle can survive for long without local leaders who know the terrain and can coordinate strategy among the people.

Within each faction one will find a number of high-ranking leaders who seem aware of the weaknesses of the Afghan resistance, and during 1980 several groups agreed to start training programs for local organizers. And yet few found it important enough to implement on a broad scale. The leaders seem for the most part indifferent to the political goals that are at least as important in most guerrilla struggles—or, to be more precise, in most revolutionary wars—as military goals are in conventional warfare.

What, traditionally, are these political aims? Guerrilla warfare is as old as man. Technically, it is characterized by a refusal to fight decisive, frontal battles, a preference for surprise and the harassment of the enemy. Politically, guerrilla movements have throughout history been means of rebellion and revolt: peasant revolts and religious uprisings; resistance to foreign aggression or an occupying army, particularly the army of an expanding imperial power, whether Roman, Ottoman, Napoleonic, or Russian. Guerrilla warfare has a long tradition in Central Asia and in the Caucasus, where wars of resistance have often continued for decades, little known to the outside world. The Basmachi revolt belongs firmly to this tradition.

In Europe, the emergence of modern nationalism in the

nineteenth century gave guerrilla warfare a new importance, for until then, resistance movements had been confined to local or regional dimensions. Not until the middle of the twentieth century did military harassment and sabotage take on the effective, and political, importance that it has throughout the world today. Until World War II guerrilla warfare was considered subordinate in classical military doctrine: a marginal tactic, useful perhaps for backing up the regular army but hardly decisive in winning a war.

Then, with Mao Zedong, guerrilla warfare became revolutionary war, a military means for overthrowing a political regime. There was little technical innovation either in Mao's writings or in his practice of guerrilla war. What was new were his political aims, and the conception inherited from Lenin, of the revolutionary vanguard. This was a highly original concept, a radically new way to organize people: the revolutionary vanguard mobilizing support and directing both military and political operations. It was first used widely in Asia, where the Chinese were early to recognize the revolutionary potential of the peasantry. The vanguard party spread revolutionary ideology and also encouraged discipline and sacrifice. Under its direction, the peasants became a cohesive fighting force with goals that extended beyond their own regions.

The victories of Marxist-Leninist revolutions in China in 1949 and in Vietnam in 1954 encouraged other nationalist groups to borrow the Leninist idea of the vanguard party for use throughout the world in wars that had nothing to do with the class struggle. One should not confuse ideology and organizational tactics: the label "Leninist" was applied often to any political groups devoted to mobilizing the population with propaganda and indoctrination, emphasis on disciplined cohesion, etcetera. These techniques, fashioned initially to advance the proletarian revolution, were thus put to use by nationalist groups throughout the Third World.

(Another, secondary, factor in the political success of modern revolutionary wars is the disruption in the global balance of power caused by Germany and Japan during World War II. Japan's attempt to dominate eastern Asia, for example, prepared the way for guerrilla victories in China and Vietnam by overturning the semicolonial order in the Far East and thus indirectly encouraging local nationalism.)

Modern guerrilla movements have taken advantage of the opportunity to negotiate with democratic Western powers: the Algerians with France, the Vietnamese with the United States. But such victories are not possible in all circumstances. In a liberal democracy, the weight of public opinion may allow some leeway for negotiation, as long as the issues at stake are not crucial to the national interest. But guerrilla movements cannot negotiate at all with dictators, whether totalitarian or not, or in case of an internal struggle against an oppressive regime. The colonies of Portuguese Africa did not win independence until after the fall of the fascist government in Lisbon. The Hungarian insurrection in Budapest in 1956 was crushed by Soviet tanks. In Cuba, as in Nicaragua, neither Castro's supporters nor the Sandinistas could hope for victory before the collapse of Batista's government or the Somoza dynasty.

Viewed in this light, the Afghan resistance can be seen to be a prisoner of its own weaknesses, which are considerable, but also of the Soviet Union's political rigidity; it is virtually impossible for the Afghan rebels to achieve a political victory by negotiating with the Soviet Union.

The goals and values of most of the Afghan resistance fighters bear the stamp, as I have said, of their traditional society. The links among the country's peoples and its various resistance groups are based on old loyalties to family and tribe and to customary patrons. One might even say, with some severity, that although the rebels give armed support to a number of different political claims, in their traditional loyalties they are as much rejecting all forms of organization as forging a liberation movement in the modern sense of the term. They confuse tactical ruses with strategic planning; consider organizational discipline an unnecessary luxury; spurn any work other than actual combat as tedious or mundane, unworthy of a guerrilla fighter. (This is true particularly among the Pushtuns.) As for the religious fundamentalism of some segments of the resistance, it is a fairly weak response to the social crisis in Afghanistan.

At the same time, the various groups within the resistance have two considerable advantages. First, their strong popular support extends throughout the country and is firmly tied to local issues. Second, the rebels' morale is strong. This is extremely important, particularly if it can be maintained, because time and endurance may be decisive factors in the struggle in Afghanistan. The Soviets know this, and since the beginning they have been prepared to stay as long as necessary.

Soviet political and military strength in Afghanistan ultimately depends on its opponent's recognizing that the U.S.S.R. is invincible. And one must admire the courage of the Afghans who alone among peoples overrun by the Russians have refused to acknowledge this foreign occupation and continue to fight against all odds. In this the Afghans' traditionalism is less a weakness than a strength in that it reinforces an inherited code that encourages combativeness and courage.

But the central question for the Afghan resistance concerns

its attitude toward nationalism. Will foreign occupation encourage a national sentiment to crystallize in this still largely tribal society? Or will any emerging nationalism founder quickly on the tribal and ethnic divisions fostered by the Soviet Union?

Divisons within the Afghan population fall traditionally into three categories: (1) linguistic, between those who speak Dari and those who speak Pushtun (the resistance groups based in Peshawar use Pushtun, for example, while the ones based in Iran speak Dari); (2) religious, the Sunni majority and Shiites; (3) ethnic, between Pushtuns and the other minorities. In some instances, those tensions overlap, the conflict between the Pushtuns and Hazaras was always religious as well as ethnic. In other cases, it is intertribal, dividing the Pushtuns against themselves. None of these conflicts has been entirely resolved since the Soviet invasion, but the resistance movement has brought together Hazaras and Nuristanis, encouraging them to cooperate with Pushtuns to resist both the government and the Soviet Union. In northern Afghanistan, the Tajiks have also joined the fighting, often in collaboration with the Islamic Society of Afghanistan led by B. Rabani, which is based in Peshawar. For the most part, in rural areas at least, Afghans of diverse tribal loyalties have joined together against the regime and the occupying foreign power.

In the cities and in areas inhabited by Pushtuns, the government has had more success encouraging and taking advantage of conflicts among Afghans, particularly within the Pushtun tribes. Sabotage and other forms of resistance are not uncommon in cities like Jalalabad and Kabul, but the physical presence of the regime and supporting Soviet troops have made it difficult to mount a unified urban rebellion. (It would be interesting in this regard to analyze the revolutionary tracts called *chabnameh,* or night letters, distributed clandestinely in Kabul.)

Roused by diverse causes and often concerned above all with specific, local conflicts, the various factions of the Afghan resistance lack coordination of any significant kind. And yet whether they are within or outside the country, they are frequently similar in their goals and in the means used to achieve them. For the most part, their headquarters are across the border in Peshawar, in a region inhabited largely by Pakistani Pushtun tribes.

Three of the six major resistance movements based in Peshawar are fundamentalist Muslim groups that have actively opposed the Afghan regime since the fall of the monarchy in 1973: the Islamic Party (Hezb-e-islami), led today by Gulbudin Hekmatyar; the Islamic Party of Yunis Khalis; and the Islamic Society of Afghanistan (Jamiat-e-islami) led by B. Rabani. The best organized of these groups is Gulbudin's Islamic Party, the other two being splinter groups that broke away during the 1970s. Even before the *coup d'état* that installed Daud's republic, the Islamic Party had gone into exile in Pakistan, where it was supported by President Bhutto, and launched an insurrection against the monarchy that was crushed by the Afghan army. Most of its members are people from the countryside who have recently moved to the city; they belong to the same social class that produced the militants of the communist Khalq faction—modest middle-class teachers or low-ranking bureaucrats, ideologically close to the Muslim Brothers. But many of the top leaders of the movement—men like Professor Niazi, an important figure in the theology faculty at the University of Kabul—were executed either by Daud or by the Khalq regime; and none of the second-ranking officials such as Gulbudin, Rabani, Yunis Khalis, or Dr. Sayyef is a charismatic figure capable of holding the party together. Thus, in recent years the party has been split by personal disputes and also perhaps by quarrels about strategy and methods.

The methods of Gulbudin's Islamic Party are severe indeed: torture and execution are commonly used to deal with those who oppose the party line. The movement calls for an Islamic revolution that would have no room for traditional spiritual leaders, who are thought to be too lenient and corrupt; for modernizers with liberal Western ideas; for tribalism or nationalism, both considered too exclusive for a universal Islamic movement; or for the atheistic communism of Khalq and Parcham. Interestingly, Gulbudin's Islamic Party is the only resistance movement that Babrak Karmal and his Soviet supporters mentioned; Karmal notes that the movement's fundamentalism makes it unlikely that it will attract any large popular following. Gulbudin refused to join the short-lived Alliance formed in 1980 to coordinate the five other resistance movements in Peshawar (Sayyef was its president); and he continues to point to Khomeini's Iran as a model for his Islamic revolution. Gulbudin is generally considered the most intelligent, ambitious, and ruthless resistance leader in Peshawar. His movement has important cells in Kabul and several northeastern provinces of Afghanistan, including Kunduz, Baghlan, Kunar, and Nangrahar.

The Islamic Party of Yunis Khalis is a regional movement, well rooted in Nangrahar province and spreading in Paktia. Khalis is the only rebel leader who takes part himself in hand-to-hand combat. The Islamic Society of Afghanistan led by Rabani is less exclusive than Gulbudin's movement, although no less strict in its fundamentalism. It is strongest in the northern provinces: in Badakhshan, Takhar, Kunduz, Baghlan, and in the Tajik regions of Samangan. (Rabani himself is a native of Badakhshan.) Rebels in the provinces to the south belong for the most part to Rabani's Islamic Society, which held the Panchir valley against frequent Soviet attacks throughout 1980.

The three other resistance movements based in Peshawar were formed during 1978–79 to combat the Khalq regime. They are

- The National Front for Islamic Revolution in Afghanistan (Payman-e-ittehad-e-islami), led by S. A. Gailani.
- The National Front for the Liberation of Afghanistan (Jabha-e-azadi-e-Afghanistan) of S. Mojadedi.
- The Islamic Revolutionary Movement (Harakat-e-inquelab-e-islami) led by Mohammad Nabi Mohamedi.

Both Gailani and Mojadedi come from prominent families of Muslim leaders and wield a traditional spiritual authority. Gailani's father came to Kabul from Baghdad, was a favorite of the Afghan King Amanullah who ruled during the 1920s, and was thought to be descended from the prophet Mohammad—an aura passed in part at least to his son. For his part, Mojadedi has come into power as the heir of his uncle Hazerat Mojadedi, a highly respected religious figure executed by the Khalqi.

Although both Gailani and Mojadedi's movements claim to be "national" fronts, they are in fact regional groups, not at the moment, at least, sufficiently strong to command a larger following. Nor are their leaders particularly dynamic, although Mojadedi is generally considered more intelligent than Gailani. Lacking internal cohesion and central organization, both movements rely on tribal allegiances among rural Pushtun groups in southern Afghanistan. None of these tribal groups fights outside its own region, and the arms they receive from headquarters in Peshawar are often inefficiently distributed and used. The fronts tend to be conservative in religious matters; but paradoxically they are also more open than Gulbudin's group to the ideas of modernizers and nationalists. The Islamic Revolutionary Movement of M. N. Mohamedi is composed largely of *mullahs,* the very group that Gulbudin's Islamic Party hopes to supersede and eventually destroy.

Mohammad Nabi Mohamedi's Islamic Revolutionary Movement (Harakat) is perhaps the largest rebel organization. Most of the *mullahs* who belong to it reject religious fundamentalism, which has in any case little appeal among the rural population. It is by definition a religious movement, and it has roots in both the north and the south of the country, its strongest outposts being in Logar, Ghazni, Baghlan, Kunduz, Kabul, and Kandahar provinces, and it extends even into western Afghanistan. But Mohamedi, who was a parliamentary representative from Logar province, does not have the authority to lead a vast movement or control its organization; and already internal factions (such as the one led by Mawlewi Nasserollah) threaten to break away from the group to form resistance movements of their own.

Both the Nuristani and Hazara tribes have their own resistance movements. The Nuristani groups are regional in organization: there are three groups of elected representatives from Laghman, Petch, and Kamdesh which together form the Nuristani Front (Jabha-e-Nuristan). The Kamdesh group has its headquarters in Peshawar, but the front's influence does not reach beyond the Kamdesh valley. The Hazaras too have elected delegates to an exiled resistance organization with cells in Iran as well as Peshawar. An isolated mountain people, the Hazaras have also organized a network of local resistance groups with front headquarters in Hazarajat—leaders who maintain communication with Nuristani rebels and occasionally cooperate with the Nuristani Front.

Other rebel organizations proclaim radical revolutionary ideologies. They are found for the most part in Kabul and other cities and have little following in rural areas. The best known is SAMA, the Organization for the Liberation of the People of Afghanistan (Sazema-e-azadibakhch-e-mardom-e-Afghanistan), which was founded in 1978 by former members of the Eternal Flame (Shula-e-Jawid), a group active in Badakhshan province. The popular founder of SAMA, Abdul Majid Kalakani, was arrested in Kabul in February 1980 and executed by the regime. SAMA claims to be a unified national front, but its influence among the people is difficult to measure, and it is unlikely that it extends outside Kabul. The same is true of the Front of Modjahid Rebels, which claims to unite five organizations under a banner of progressive Islam. In reality, the Sunnite Islam of most Afghans remains untouched by any reform or innovation, and those who argue for Islamic renewal belong to a tiny vanguard within an extremely limited group.

Yet another militant group, the Afghan People's Organization, claims to represent revolutionary workers and peasants, but it too is largely urban in its following, based in Jalalabad. Its leader is the former member of parliament Feda Mohammad Fedan. The National Islamic Revolution of the Afghan People (Itihad-i-inqelab-i-islamwa Afghan Milli) is a socialist organization based in Peshawar and led by G. M. Ferhat. Often called simply Afghan Milli, it is a small Pushtun-speaking group of devoted fighters without means and without a social base. When it tried to establish a cell in Nangrahar province, it was brutally crushed by Yunis Khalis's Islamic Party, which found the socialists too radical and insufficiently religious. A traditional institution, the Loya Jirga, was elected in the countryside during the summer of 1980 but was manipulated by S. A. Gailani from Peshawar, although he and his lieutenants from the National Front met with little success. Still, a more representative Loya Jirga could in the future provide the badly needed link between exiled leaders in Peshawar and discontented rebels fighting inside Afghanistan.

Western leftists are often tempted to back small, urban rebel movements that support a revolutionary ideology. The Afghan resistance is thus recognized and applauded as a "national liberation movement" with revolutionary goals. But in truth the revolutionary factions within the resistance are, and are certain to remain, a tiny minority. None of the major Afghan rebel groups with popular followings stands to the left of Babrak Karmal's regime. On the contrary, the movement is for the most part regionally based and only regionally ambitious; it draws its strength from two essentially conservative groups, either religious fundamentalists supported more or less by neighboring Islamic countries, or Islamic nationalists who at best can only steer the movement toward the relatively modern goal of nationalism.

Babrak Karmal can hardly pretend that his regime, supported as it is by Soviet troops, represents Afghan nationalism. Thanks to the Soviet intervention, the resistance movement can hope to channel popular resentment into a recognizably nationalist movement. Certainly, it is unlikely that the Afghan resistance will meet with much long-range success if it does not draw on and encourage nationalism, creating at least among its cadres a sense of modern political goals. Until now, however, the movement has not been able to take advantage of a nationalist current.

Afghanistan stands at a point of crisis, waiting for badly

needed economic growth and social progress. Unlike the DPPA of Babrak Karmal, the fundamentalist rebels can deliver neither. Determined above all not to reinforce or encourage religious feeling, the regime defends Islamic modernism.

But the Afghan people violently reject the imposition of "socialism" by foreign troops supporting an unpopular regime. For them religion is an ideology of resistance, a cornerstone of group identity. Thus many rebel leaders from Kabul who rejected all religious practice only two years ago now make a show of taking time out for the five daily Islamic prayers.

Afghan nationalism remains for the moment a weak and uncertain movement, mainly because Afghans' loyalties are religious, ethnic, and tribal. But in Afghanistan as elsewhere, foreign domination in this era may prepare fertile ground for the seeds of modern nationalism.

5 SOVIET STRATEGY AND AFGHAN RESPONSE

So far, the Russians have played their hand well. They have avoided the mistake made by the French in Algeria and by the Americans in Vietnam—the mistake of trying to occupy a country with an expeditionary force of some 500,000 men—and they have not been burdened with an enormous force of largely unneeded soldiers who would have been expensive to feed, and of whom only 10–15 percent would have been useful in combat. Instead the Soviets have chosen, whether for political or economic reasons, to send only 85,000 men into Afghanistan—just enough to control the cities and principal roads.

Since 1978, nearly half of the 80,000 men of the Afghan army have deserted to join the resistance, often taking their arms and even their ammunition. But the soldiers who remain have been able to hold the dense line of fortified posts that the government maintains on the Pakistani border. During 1980, mines were planted around these camps and the poorly armed resistance can do little to sabotage them. Still, the regular soldiers of the Afghan army, imprisoned in these isolated forts, undoubtedly feel harassed by the rebels' hazing—inefficient as it may be.

Soviet troops move around the country in armored columns that are largely invulnerable to rebel attacks. The resistance have few antitank guns, and most of the mines they have used until now have been of such poor quality that they are rarely able to damage a tank. When a column of tanks is attacked, the Soviets intervene quickly with MI-24 helicopters to counter the rebels.

One rarely sees Soviet soldiers outside of Kabul and the other major cities. The cautious general staff is determined to avoid risks, and for the most part the troops live in isolated barracks and move around in armored vehicles. In the cities, they are rarely vulnerable except when they are on leave—for soldiers separated from their regiments are often attacked by urban terrorists, particularly in Kabul.

I saw few airborne Soviet troops in Afghanistan, although it is likely that they will be used increasingly to counter attacks by resistance fighters. They were first brought in during the summer of 1980 to sabotage guerrilla encampments in Kunar province. Camps were surrounded and heavily bombed before helicopters dropped parachute troops on neighboring hills. After the prolonged bombardment, cleanup operations were generally fast and effective.

During the first six months of 1980, the Russians were concerned above all to control the Pakistani border region, particularly Kunar and Paktia and, to a lesser degree, Ghazni provinces. The resistance is fairly strong in this region, and the mujahedeen responded in kind to the army's attacks. But Soviet and Afghan troops caused a significant part of the peasant population to flee from their homes in the border region and throughout the eastern part of the country: between

1979 and 1980 the number of Afghan refugees in Pakistan grew from 400,000 to 1,400,000. Many of them were driven out by Soviet bombing aimed directly at the civilian population or at their fields and workshops and warehouses. Others left because of rumors that spread panic throughout the countryside. Some peasants took their families to safety across the border and then returned to their villages to work the fields; in the meantime, fellow tribesmen took turns caring for absent neighbors' plots. In Kunar province, I also saw abandoned villages: the houses were intact but empty, the fields unharvested, even at the end of October. Soviet troops have also planted antipersonnel mines throughout the eastern region of the country, greatly adding to the guerrillas' logistical problems.

According to the United Nations High Commission for Refugees, by March 15, 1981, more than 2 million Afghans had crossed the border into Pakistan. This figure may be somewhat exaggerated, since it is unlikely that as many as 600,000 refugees would make the difficult trip through the mountains during the three winter months. But it is clear that the Soviets have achieved their strategic goal: guerrillas traveling through the depopulated border region can rarely rely on local peasants to shelter or feed them. Like all counterinsurgent forces, the Russians work at "generating refugees"— as the Americans did in Vietnam—and driving peasants from the countryside into the cities. Thus, the occupying army tries to empty out the water in order to kill the fish. Several Afghan cities grew considerably during 1980: Jalalabad (capital of Nangrahar province), Ghazni, Gardez, Khost (in Paktia), Charikar (in Parwan), and others. Ninety percent of the refugees driven across the Pakistani border are Pushtun, and most of them came from the frontier provinces of Kunar, Nangrahar, Paktia, Ghazni, Badakhshan, Logar, and Kandahar.

Some 150,000 refugees have also crossed into Iran, most of them from the western province of Herat. Once the border region has been emptied, Soviet troops will probably try to create a buffer zone in the hills along the Pakistani frontier—a no-man's-land where guerrillas are easily tracked and caught.

The Soviet troops and the regime they installed in power have had some success in organizing the tribal people in the eastern mountains. In order to gain the allegiance of tribal chiefs who, for various reasons, were unsympathetic to the rebels, the Russians made payments to Muslim groups in Kunar, to the Shinwari tribe in Nangrahar, and the Mangal and Jaji tribes in Paktia. Not surprisingly, this cooperation has created difficulties for the resistance. But as long as no blood has been shed, it is still possible, according to Afghan tradition, for these tribes to realign themselves with the resistance forces.

Tribal allegiances are traditionally fragile and changeable, determined by the shifting interests of the group. And it is quite possible that circumstances will disrupt existing alliances between local headmen and the regime. At the same time, the regime has taken full advantage of its alliances with various tribal chiefs, boasting of their cooperation in order to gain increased support among people in the towns. This policy occasionally backfires: Faiz Mohammad, minister of tribal affairs, was assassinated in the summer of 1980 in Paktia during negotiations with tribal leaders. But it seems likely that the regime will continue to woo important chiefs and to rely on their support. Of course, in strategically important regions where the "graybeards" choose not to cooperate, the regime will simply bombard the population, "generating refugees" and undermining the resistance in traditional strongholds such as Kunar, Paktia, Wardak, and Logar provinces.

But for the most part, Soviet activity has been concentrated in the cities, particularly in Kabul. The Soviets were concerned above all to impose order by building up the administrative organization of the Parcham faction and occasionally replacing Parcham functionaries with Soviet administrators. The task of governing has been considerably complicated by the rivalry between Khalq and Parcham factions and by the narrowness of the social strata that support the regime. Still, the Russians have been able to push through a number of administrative reforms. In the summer of 1980, special identity cards were distributed to merchants in Kabul to help the government control travel into and out of the city. These measures have also helped prevent resistance fighters from infiltrating the bazaar, although the guerrillas maintain a network of supporters among city merchants and in certain units of the regular army.

What does the Soviet Union hope to achieve in Afghanistan? In part it expects to draw the country into its economic sphere, taking advantage of unexploited and underexploited natural resources like oil, uranium, chrome, manganese, copper, coal, iron, and semiprecious stones. It also intends to create new jobs for the young unemployed people in the towns. Thus, during 1979 and 1980, the Soviets launched a number of economic projects to strengthen the industrial infrastructure of Afghanistan and increase its trade with Russia. It will require considerable time to isolate the Afghan guerrilla forces and to develop the Afghan economy, but eventually the Russians hope to produce a new social class within Afghanistan that will accept and even support the new regime. Thus they want, with time, to vindicate the regime.

These, then, are the broad lines of Soviet strategy in Afghanistan. Its cost, until now, has been very moderate. The Russians have lost little equipment, and the estimates of casualties announced by the resistance and by "diplomatic sources" in New Delhi have been considerably exaggerated. Some reports picked up by the Western press have suggested, for example, that in September 1980 alone the Soviet army lost 1500 men. This seems highly unlikely, given that in a decade of guerrilla war against well-armed Vietnamese forces, the United States lost only 50,000 men. Most reasonable estimates suggest that the Soviet army in Afghanistan lost no more than 2000 to 4000 men during all of 1980.

Only a Western press unfamiliar with the war in Afghanistan could announce, as several papers did in June 1980, that the resistance was preparing to attack Kabul. By the same token, the inflated language of Westerners who talk about "genocide" in Afghanistan helps no one on either side. Although at one time the Western press tended to overestimate the guerrilla forces, it has now become fashionable to express a more disparaging view. What is not said in these more skeptical accounts is that few other resistance groups, whether Asian, African, or Latin American, have had to fight under such unequal conditions. Also unnoticed, and even more important now, is the fact that the morale of the Afghan resistance has not been broken. The insurgents have not yet suffered a fierce, unrelenting attack like the antiguerrilla campaign in which General Challe destroyed the Willayas in Algeria in 1958 and 1959, or the "search and destroy" missions and Phoenix operation that the United States carried out in Vietnam in 1969 and 1970.

In Afghanistan, for the time being, the outcome of the fighting remains uncertain. The regime still cannot count on much support among the people, even in the cities. It has not yet been able to recruit enough young men to maintain an army of 40,000 fighters, although by Afghan standards army wages are considered good. (A noncommissioned officer earns 6,000 afghanis—about $120, a militiaman 3,000–4,000 afghanis—about $90 a month.) On several occasions students have organized street demonstrations against the regime. Moreover, a large part of the educated class was killed in the various purges conducted by rival factions during the period from 1978 to 1980. Other important administrators have refused to collaborate with the new regime, and many skilled and educated people have left the country—an erosion of the professional classes that has undermined regime and resistance alike. Today, both sides lack political leaders and technicians.

How has the resistance fared since the invasion? The movement has not been broken, but the insurgents are still badly organized and much divided among themselves. They are sustained largely by their own aggressive determination, the product of their tribal culture and its warrior traditions. But not even their commitment to their cause can make up for their debilitating lack of arms. Proud of their independent tradition and inspired by their warrior ideal, the Afghan guerrillas continue to fight in the face of odds that would deter most other peoples. They simply do not know the habit of submission. The Soviet intervention of December 27, 1979, was the first attempt since the Anglo-Afghan wars made by any foreign power to overrun Afghanistan with an occupying force. The rebels continue to fight in the flamboyant style of traditional tribal warriors—showing a kind of personal heroism that can be effective in isolated incidents but that also tends to prevent the kind of efficient military organization that a successful resistance movement must, in the end, have.

That the Afghan insurgents know little of modern revolutionary war—its efficiency or organization or careful planning of time and work—is not surprising, but sadly ironic, given that one of their central goals is to preserve their culture from the incursions of the centralized, modern state.

Although they lack organization and coordinated strategy, the guerrillas have concentrated their fighting along two geographic lines of resistance. One runs east-west, cutting through the middle of the country from the Pakistan border to Hazarajat, at the very center of Afghanistan. The other runs north-south, outlining the eastern half of the country and ending in its central region. Outside these two vast mountain regions (which cover more than half of Afghanistan), the guerrillas have established strongholds in the areas around Kandahar and Herat.* There are only a few insurgents in northwestern Afghanistan or its semidesert zones.

In certain areas, the Russians have tolerated open dissidence among the peasants. The central region, for example, is without strategic importance, and in such areas, the resistance generally remains local and autonomous, though with significant links to insurgents in other parts of the country. The Hazara are also active in Kabul, where they migrate to work as porters and unskilled laborers.

Only the six resistance movements with headquarters in Peshawar are recognized by the Pakistani government as official representatives of the refugees that have crossed the border from Afghanistan. This means that only they can receive whatever money and supplies are contributed from abroad, and they control the distribution of such aid in the interior of Afghanistan. It also means that groups like the Free Mujahedeen and other small independent bands fighting in-

---

* Although the Parcham faction is said to hold the old city of Herat, the newer part of town apparently eludes their control. Commandos trained in Iran operate throughout the region.

side Afghanistan have little chance of developing if they have no links with the six movements recognized by Pakistan.

But while the larger movements often compete for whatever foreign aid is available, their local organizations sometimes overlap and frequently cooperate in the field. Thus, in the competition for aid, Gulbudin's Islamic Party has won the support of Iran, while the nonfundamentalists are backed by Egypt. Within Afghanistan, however, even when they cooperate, one of the resistance groups usually dominates the others: Yunis Khalis's Islamic Party largely controls the fighting in Nangrahar province, while the Islamic Society is stronger in Panchir, and Gailani's National Front has gained supremacy in Wardak.

As for geographical strategy, the resistance aims above all to keep an access open to the mountainous frontier regions whence it can descend into the interior of the country: the northern hills that give onto Badakhshan and Nuristan, and the southern border zone that gives access to Paktia. In the same way, Logar and Wardak provinces give the insurgents a route into Kabul, and the southern province of Kandahar could provide an important strategic base. In the coming months, the provinces of Parwan, Takhar, Kunduz, Kunar, and Nangrahar will also be bitterly disputed. At the same time, rebel strategy must take careful account of the seasons, since little fighting takes place in the mountains during the winter—from the end of October to the end of April—and large coordinated operations are generally possible only between May and October.

Until now, the resistance has used only three relatively simple types of operation: sabotaging the roads, skirmishes outside the forts and fortified villages held by the regular army, and terrorist strikes in the towns. Thus it seems likely that the insurgents will fight in smaller, mobile commando bands. But only if they are better armed will they be able to improve and increase their harassment of Soviet vehicles.

Lack of arms and ammunition is the rebels' most pressing problem—although in comparison with their lack of organization, the problem of weaponry is relatively easy to overcome. The guerrillas are still fighting with British Lee-Enfield rifles left over from World War II and with Kalashnikov automatic weapons made in Egypt. Kalashnikovs are available on the Pakistani market for about $1400 each (equivalent to more than ten times the monthly salary of a noncom in the regular Afghan army—considered quite a good salary by Afghan standards), but they are still in great demand inside Afghanistan. Deserters from the regular army bring the rebels RPK, PK, and PKS machine guns; the resistance has also acquired a very small number of RPG 7 Soviet antitank guns and a few cannons without recoil mechanisms or mortar. Against helicopters, they use a few heavy machine guns made in China as well as perhaps half a dozen SAM 7 ground-to-air missiles.

But certainly there is little evidence to support the Soviet allegations that the rebels are receiving arms from the West. To my knowledge, Egypt is the only state that has given them any kind of light weapons, and only Saudi Arabia and the Gulf Emirates have provided financial aid.

The Afghan resistance movements have not yet been able to take advantage of public opinion in Europe or the United States. For the most part, they know little of the world outside Afghanistan and do not recognize how important such public sympathy could be. It can only be a matter of time, however, before Westerners begin to recognize them as a people fighting for their liberty. Thus the resistance movements must continue to publicize their cause.

But the guerrillas' prospects still depend above all on acquiring heavy antitank and antiaircraft weapons as well as mines and other explosives to replace the mediocre ones currently in use in Afghanistan.

Although until now the invasion of Afghanistan has had few diplomatic repercussions for the Soviet Union, an American decision to send aid to the resistance movements would considerably raise the stakes for the U.S.S.R. It is unlikely that the Russians would be willing to negotiate about Afghanistan itself, but their presence there could become a bargaining chip or a point of leverage for the United States— something to be traded for concessions in other areas as part of a diplomatic "package deal." If this were to happen, American aid to the resistance would only strengthen Washington's hand—although of course the negotiations would have little benefit for the Afghan resistance itself.

In the meantime, in any case, the rebels have little choice but to go on fighting. In the short run at least, the outcome will depend above all on their determination and tenacity. They have not as yet shown any signs of faltering resolve, but their poor organization and lack of cohesion continue to weaken them badly.

6 CONCLUSION

The Soviet Union, unlike Western colonial powers, has not given up its efforts to expand its empire: it does this by conquering neighboring rather than overseas territories. Under the Tsarist regime, during the eighteenth and nineteenth centuries, Russia expanded southward as far as the Caucasus and eastward, or southeastward, as far as Central Asia and Vladivostok.* After the revolution, in 1920–21, the U.S.S.R. annexed Georgia and Armenia as well as the emirate of Bukhara. Following World War II, the Soviet Union took advantage of victory to annex not only the Baltic states (Estonia, Lithuania, and Latvia) but also territory that had previously been part of Finland (Karelia), Rumania (Bessarabia), Germany (eastern Prussia), Poland, and Czechoslovakia. These new boundaries and the new territory that the U.S.S.R. acquired in central and western Europe at the close

---

* 1783, the conquest of the Crimea and Kuban; 1859, the Caucasus; 1865, Tashkent; 1868, the khanate of Samarkand; 1876, the khanate of Kokand; 1884, the khanate of Merv; 1885, the khanate of Pundjeh and Aktepa; 1896, Pamir.

of World War II were confirmed by the Helsinki Conference in 1975.

In the Soviets' view, only an aggressive foreign policy will guarantee national security; and thanks to its growing military power, Moscow is now able to control a larger area than ever before, particularly in regions that border on the Soviet Union itself.

Since the beginning of the Cold War, the U.S.S.R. has demonstrated several times that it will brook no opposition in central Europe: in East Berlin in 1953, Budapest in 1956, Czechoslovakia in 1968. During this period, its only significant setback was the break with Yugoslavia in 1948. (The conflict with China is an entirely different kind of reversal— hardly a rupture between patron and client state.) Since the late 1940s, the Soviets' only serious diplomatic setback was the expulsion of their diplomats, technicians, and military personnel from Egypt in 1972.*

What is new, and largely unnoticed, about Soviet foreign policy today is that many of the regimes that it supports have come to depend for their very survival on the presence of Soviet or Cuban troops. This has been true in Southern Yemen since the mid-1970s; it is true in Angola and in Ethiopia. The Ethiopians have perhaps the greatest chance of cutting loose from Moscow in the years to come, but the MPLA (Popular Movement for the Liberation of Angola) government in Angola has very little room to maneuver around South Africa's active support of the rival Unita movement.

As for Afghanistan, it is without question one of the most useful of Russia's outposts outside its own territory. Certainly it is unlikely that Afghanistan will be able to shake free of

---

* The upheaval in Poland is not a diplomatic setback but, rather, a fundamental rejection of the Soviet system. The Cuban missile crisis was also a wholly different kind of upset.

Soviet control. Both the Soviet military presence and Afghanistan's geographical position—next to the U.S.S.R. and China, and on the Soviet route to the Persian Gulf—virtually rule out such a reversal. Although opposition is widespread and Babrak Karmal's regime lacks a significant base of support, the Russians themselves have no competition there. It is generally acknowledged that Afghanistan falls within the Russian geopolitical orbit; only the invasion of December 1979 was needed to bring it directly under Soviet control. Of course, this would not have been tolerated at a time when American political will was stronger or even before the fall of the Shah of Iran. Indeed, it is only tolerated now because most Western diplomats are uncertain about its significance. Is it the first step in a more ambitious regional strategy that will quickly prove unacceptable to the West? Or is it a contained local maneuver best described by the American term "Afghan specific"? If the latter turns out to be the case, most Western governments will probably decide that, whatever it means for the Afghan people, they can avert their eyes. This is the Soviet wager—and so far the game is going their way.

The emphasis that the Soviet Union has put on maintaining peaceful relations with the West since the intervention in Afghanistan demonstrates once again that peaceful coexistence is largely compatible with competition between East and West. The Soviet Union has rarely pretended otherwise: peaceful coexistence and competition, particularly in the Third World, are two prongs of a single policy designed to take advantage of the adversary whenever possible.

The Russians have used shrewd diplomacy and considerable political skill in handling the international response to their intervention in Afghanistan. Already in the period between the *coup d'état* of April 1978 and the military intervention in December 1979, they had used their influence with the regime in Kabul to alter radically Afghanistan's traditional position as a neutral buffer state. It was during that period, in February 1979, that the American ambassador to Kabul was kidnapped and killed by Afghan guerrillas; and even then, the American reaction was surprisingly muffled. Later, American public opinion was entirely preoccupied by the Iranians' holding their diplomats hostage in Teheran.

Thus the Russians continue to pursue a "Marxist-Leninist" foreign policy—a program that of course has little connection with the beliefs of most Soviet citizens, who are all too aware of the yawning gaps between political-economic reality and government ideology. In this, the regime has chosen to ignore the consequences that such an aggressive policy may have for the already somewhat tarnished image of socialism.

In explaining the intervention, people often refer to Soviet fears of a fundamentalist revolution that would begin among the Islamic peoples of Russia and then spread across the border to those elsewhere in Central Asia.*

There are some 45 million Muslims living inside the Soviet Union. Some belong to ethnic groups, like the Kazaks, that are wholly contained within Soviet borders. Others, like the Uzbeks, Turkomen, and Tajiks, have relatives across the frontier in northern Afghanistan. Altogether they account for some 18 percent of the Soviet population, but as a group they are growing considerably faster than the Slavic population of the U.S.S.R. (Thus, during the past twenty years, the Slavic population has grown by 5 percent while the Muslim groups have grown by close to 25 percent. Twenty years from now, the Muslim population will have virtually doubled.)

But how are these Muslims regarded by the Russians, and

---

* This is largely an oversimplified reading of the valuable scholarly work of Hélène Carrère d'Encausse, *L'Empire éclaté* (Paris, 1978).

what kind of position do they hold in Soviet society? Ethnic and religious prejudice is common and reciprocal. Soviet Muslims have achieved considerable economic and cultural development; many are well educated and technologically sophisticated.

Scholars such as Alexandre Bennigsen and Chantal Lemercier-Quelquejay have refuted the popular Western notion that Soviet Muslims are a poorly educated or disenfranchised group. In truth these groups boast an intellectual elite with technical and political skills as sophisticated as those of their Russian neighbors. Although they have not been able to penetrate the army or the secret police, both still wholly controlled by Russians, Soviet Muslims are well represented in their own local governments and in the administrations of the republics where they are concentrated. Moreover, local Muslim leaders tend to reinforce their places in both government and party with traditional family and tribal loyalties. And unlike Russian intellectuals and politicians, they generally maintain good relations with the population as a whole: for the most part, Soviet Muslims recognize local leaders as their representatives and even look to them for political guidance. But they remain strongly attached to Islamic customs and generally seem to take their identity from the historical past—Islamic history and two centuries of resistance against Russian culture.* Recently, they have also experienced a religious revival, in both the modern, progressive branch of Islam and in the fundamentalist Sufi brotherhood. It is hardly surprising, then, that Muslims living in the U.S.S.R. are greatly interested in the Muslim societies of neighboring Asian countries like Iran and Turkey.

---

* See Alexandre Bennigsen and Chantal Lemercier-Quelquejay, "L'Expérience soviétique en pays musulman: les leçons du passé et l'Afghanistan," *Politique étrangère* (Paris, July 1980).

At this stage it would be foolish to expect that the Muslim elites, whether communist or religious, will bring about the disintegration of the Soviet empire. Far from wanting to destroy the regime, for the moment they cooperate with it in a number of ways. In this, they are generally guided by the rules of *bazarlik* [literally, "haggling"]—a complicated game in which each player is obliged to make concessions—although certainly the Muslim elites hope to be the principal beneficiaries of the game. At present, there is virtually no organized opposition in the Muslim republics apart from the Sufi brotherhood, which is strongest in the northern Caucasus. There is no Moslem *samizdat,* and the only ethnic protest, vehement or otherwise, that one hears in the Soviet Union comes from two deported nationalities: the Crimean Tatars and the Turks of Maskhetia.*

Still, it would be wrong to underestimate the threat that the Muslim minorities in the Soviet Union pose for the regime. Their religious renewal, their self-conscious concern for the past, their unusually high rate of demographic growth—all of these make their future highly uncertain. A nationalist movement will undoubtedly develop. Indeed, the Muslim peoples of the Central Asian Soviet republic may feel that the intervention in Afghanistan strengthened the Islamic presence in the Soviet orbit. Certainly, the Soviet government was extremely eager to replace the Asian soldiers who took part in the advance into Afghanistan. But then, this could mean anything; it is, after all, a familiar Soviet tactic, also used in Czechoslovakia in 1968.

Only eighteen months after the intervention, the Soviet regime seems to have overcome whatever diplomatic embarrassment it incurred. Even in early 1980, the American reaction to the invasion hardly amounted to a tenth of the

---

* Bennigsen and Lemercier-Quelquejay, p. 79.

outrage aroused by the Iranians' taking of the hostages in Teheran. We live in a world where a white skin is still more valuable than any other kind. And in the United States, as throughout the world, much of the protest against the action in Afghanistan has faded with time. The reaction of other Muslim countries was bitter at first, but before long they too backed down, unable to reach a consensus about how to protest to the Soviet Union. Of course, many Arab countries are linked to Russia by trade or other economic cooperation, and together they found that it is easier to agree on a resolution demanding rights for Palestinians than to oppose the Russians by supporting the Afghan resistance. Europe was far from eager to confront the Soviets, provoking a crisis over a local maneuver that seemed unlikely to go beyond Afghanistan. In this, the West Germans were particularly cautious, concerned above all to protect their *Ostpolitik* and their growing trade with the Soviet Union. As a result, the U.S.S.R. has been able to define its presence in Afghanistan as a narrow, regional issue, of little concern to anyone but the two neighboring countries, Iran and Pakistan. Between them, the Russians hope to act as arbiter, ignoring their own traditional bias in the region and largely controlling the diplomatic game in order to reinforce their own influence on their southern flank.

Of course, much depends on the response of the Reagan administration. The Republicans are expected to support the Afghan resistance with either financial aid or heavy weapons, thus considerably raising the stakes of the conflict in Afghanistan. But American concern about instability in Iran and Pakistan, in the Persian Gulf and the Indian Ocean, will undoubtedly prevent President Reagan from provoking an international crisis over Afghanistan.

Besides, whatever aid is given to the resistance, Afghani-

stan will not become a Soviet "Vietnam." The South Vietnamese FLN relied on active and organized support from
North Vietnam—an ally that came to participate more and
more in the war going on in the south. The Soviet Union and
China contributed a considerable amount of aid. Finally, of
course, after 1968 and 1969, American public opinion was increasingly opposed to the distant and apparently unwinnable
war in Southeast Asia. In this, the Soviet Union has a significant advantage over the United States: the absence of public
opinion as a force in politics. Of course, international public
opinion and diplomatic pressures sometimes substitute for
domestic public opinion in a totalitarian state. But public
concern about military losses in Afghanistan will never
threaten the Soviet regime or affect the outcome of the fighting there. In this sense, the U.S.S.R. has time on its side, and
in this case, unlike Vietnam, time could prove to be decisive.
This is not to say that the Soviet regime might not be severely
weakened if the resistance was tenacious enough to bring
about a long stalemate. That is, of course, an uncertain bet.
But at the moment, at least, the Afghan resistance has no political alternative.

The regional neighbor most threatened by the Soviet presence in Afghanistan is undoubtedly Pakistan: an unstable
state with an enormous foreign debt, largely without a national identity or hope of economic development. Pakistani
agriculture is extremely backward, its industry is hopelessly
inefficient, and the government in Islamabad rules without
popular support. Such is the precarious state that provides
sanctuary for the Afghan resistance. General Zia-ul-Haq has
ruled Pakistan since 1977, when he was brought to power by a
coup d'état. But even today his militry regime remains very
fragile, caught in a complicated economic bind: in large part
it depends for its survival on the good will of the United

States and a recent decision by the World Bank to reschedule its debt; other aid came from the International Monetary Fund, which in 1980 granted it a $1.7 billion loan that will not come due until 1983. Yet all of this is merely oxygen for a country in crisis, temporary relief rather than a lasting cure.

Pakistan was created in 1947, a Muslim state carved from the Indian empire. Pakistanis were never happy with the division and even today they continue to lay claim to the disputed territory of Kashmir. But in more than thirty years their demands have come to nothing except a continued rivalry with India. In the meantime, India has become a considerable military power with a nuclear bomb. It has also been able to weaken its Muslim neighbor severely by helping to create Bangladesh in the region that was once eastern Pakistan.

When General Zia came to power in 1977, he first jailed and then executed Ali Bhutto, the former leader of the country, "suspended" all political parties, silenced his political opponents, and repeatedly postponed elections. Not surprisingly, his policies have wreaked havoc, compounding the ethnic rivalries that traditionally divide the country. The Punjabis are the dominant people, accounting for approximately 60 percent of the population. Other major groups include the Pushtun, Baluchi, and Sindhi peoples, who occupy some 70 percent of the land—most of it admittedly desert.

The Baluchis, the smallest group but also the most dissident, have for many years been fighting for autonomy from Pakistan, and at one time they enjoyed the support of both Afghanistan and the Soviet Union. They have made common cause with Baluchis in Iran and Afghanistan, and their "separatism" continues to pose a grave threat to the unity of Pakistan: this is a trump card that the U.S.S.R. could play at any time to force the Pakistani government to reduce or cut off the foreign aid that sustains the Afghan resistance. At the moment, there are some 50,000 Pakistani troops stationed in the Baluchi region, and the separatist movement is badly weakened by tribal divisions. Still, it is clear that it would be difficult for the Pakistani economy to withstand a revival of Baluchi unrest.

Relations between the United States and Pakistan have improved notably, in large part in reaction to the Soviet presence in Afghanistan. The Pakistanis have traditionally maintained good relations with Washington, although the friendship had been in decline since the war between India and Pakistan in 1965, when the United States cut off all military aid. Since then, India has pursued an unrestrained nuclear policy, while Pakistan has been severely criticized, particularly by President Carter, for trying to develop a similar program. Relations with Washington deteriorated even further in December 1979, after the Pakistani attack on the American embassy in Islamabad.

Shortly after the Soviet intervention in Afghanistan, the United States offered Pakistan a $400 million aid package. President Zia refused it, on the grounds that this was too modest a sum. In June 1980, a consortium of creditor countries decided to roll over a Pakistani debt of some $5 billion, but recent loans from the World Bank and the IMF have raised the debt to some $12 billion. In this difficult situation, it is hardly surprising that Pakistan wants to take full financial advantage of its strategic position. At the end of March 1981, the United States offered Pakistan a two-year loan of $500 million along with a vague "security guarantee."

This aid from the United States, the World Bank, and the IMF may bring economic recovery to Pakistan. But the political situation there remains fragile. The government faces considerable opposition from a coalition of discontented groups, including the party that once supported President Bhutto. And of course Zia is under pressure from the Soviet Union. Kabul did not, for example, hesitate to press him to release political prisoners in the spring of 1980 when a Pakistani airplane was hijacked to Afghanistan.

In fact, the Pakistani regime is in a very difficult situation. Moscow demands that it remain "neutral" in the struggle between the Afghan government and the resistance, while the United States pays for its loyalty by guaranteeing its economic survival. Until now, Pakistan's policy has been to take as much aid as possible while doing as little as possible for the Afghan resistance. It is a difficult line, and an extremely precarious one.

China has also for many years sent considerable military aid to Pakistan. According to General Zia, whose estimates may be somewhat exaggerated, Peking provided some $2 billion in arms and ammunition between 1966 and 1980. During this period, China also undertook and completed the Karakorum-China-Pakistan road. Peking clearly has considerable interest in maintaining stability in the region and may indeed see the Afghan conflict as yet another issue on which it sides with Washington in opposition to the U.S.S.R. Thus it is not inconceivable that China may soon substantially increase its aid to the Afghan resistance.

As for Iran, its participation in the Afghan struggle—its limited aid to the Afghan rebels—is clearly less important than its strategic position. The geopolitical stakes in Iran are considerably higher, for both America and the Soviet Union, than in Afghanistan. Indeed, for Russia, the Afghan intervention is above all a means to achieve a new regional balance with Pakistan and Iran, an equilibrium keyed to the status of Afghanistan and thus largely controlled by the Soviet Union.

Although India undoubtedly fears a Soviet advance so close to its borders, it is clearly pleased to see its rival Pakistan under such enormous strain—a strain that virtually guarantees further Indian supremacy on the subcontinent. Indira Gandhi has demanded that the Russians retreat from Afghanistan and arrange for a political solution to replace its military presence. But India nevertheless maintains fairly close ties with the Soviet Union, acting as go-between for it and the nonaligned countries in exchange for considerable military aid.

The importance of the Soviet intervention in Afghanistan has been underestimated by Western public opinion and all too quickly put aside by most European leaders. We have only begun to see the consequences of either the Soviet venture or the increasingly tense East-West rivalry that it brought to light. The Russian intervention in Afghanistan marks the end of an epoch—the epoch of *détente*. Yet the Western response has from the beginning been reserved: a limited boycott of the Olympic Games in Moscow; an American embargo on grain sales to Russia, which had not much consequence because other countries such as Argentina continued to sell to the U.S.S.R.; a gradual reduction of American technological aid to Russia, which has as yet had little perceptible effect. Several West European countries that have denounced the Soviet intervention in Afghanistan continue to trade with the U.S.S.R. France, under Giscard d'Estaing, for example, even added new commercial links with Moscow.

The intervention could not have come at a more propitious time for the Soviet Union—a time of American political weakness, increasing Soviet military strength, and Russian success in other Third World countries such as Ethiopia and Angola. The Soviets also took advantage of a favorable climate in the Middle East after the fall of the Shah. But the

Russians' motives for their advance into Afghanistan, whether offensive or defensive, are much less important than the consequences of their intervention. The Soviet Union has ventured into a zone of vital importance for Western security, whether Europeans realize it or not, and its troops are ideally placed to bring about a significant shift in the regional balance of western Asia. It was, for Moscow, a shrewd and calculated risk, one that showed off technical achievement and military skill, both in the air and on the ground. The Soviets even took the West by *surprise:* a considerable military achievement.

But perhaps most troubling are the divisions that the Soviet move revealed among Western powers: Americans and Europeans still disagree about how best to cope with the intervention. The Americans' reaction was certainly inadequate— stinting their aid to the Afghan resistance fighters who continue to oppose the Soviet army. But the Europeans' response was even less satisfactory: they protested, but never so loudly as to endanger either trade with the Soviet Union or regional advantages as the middlemen of *détente.*

This reticence does not signal the "Finlandization" of Europe: France and Great Britain have nuclear weapons, and West Germany has conventional forces. But these countries' reaction to the Russian intervention in Afghanistan points unequivocally to the "provincialization" of Europe: Paris and London and Bonn seem to be renouncing any interests outside of an extremely narrow geographical sphere, a "world" limited to Africa and the Middle East. Problems in other areas are seen as distant issues for which Europe bears little responsibility, matters better left to the United States and Russia. Moreover, Europeans find, they are increasingly vulnerable to Soviet pressure: the *Ostpolitik* of West Germany has become an Achilles' heel. France and West Germany and smaller West European countries fear that they can no longer afford to renounce the economic and commercial advantages of good relations with the Soviet Union—except, perhaps, in an emergency of the gravest kind.

The Russian intervention in Afghanistan has come at a time of deep and lasting international crisis. In today's interdependent world market, such a crisis affects everyone, including those in the East, the "people's democracies" of Eastern Europe, and the countries of the Third World—sparing only a handful of oil-producing states with scant populations. No longer confident of either American nuclear supremacy or continued economic growth, Europeans and Japanese now perceive that they too are highly vulnerable to shifts in the market and dependent on oil from the Persian Gulf region. But the crisis is political as well as economic. The political dimension may be seen in growing Soviet military strength—in space, naval technology, nuclear power, and conventional troops—and in increasing tension throughout the Third World. And although it is the Soviet Union that generally seems to benefit from these changes in the world climate, in reality they result from contradictions either produced or reinforced by Western domination. This will not, of course, make it any easier for Western countries to deal with the indirect and sometimes direct confrontations that they will almost certainly face in coming years, at a time when many of them may also face considerable domestic crises. But then, of course, the West is still a relatively well-protected enclave and it is unlikely that many Westerners in any social class will experience the kind of poverty or desperate insecurity that are already common in most countries of the Third World.

In the United States, the Republican administration rode to power on a wave of popular nostalgia for the 1950s—nostalgia for the undisputed American supremacy of that lost epoch. But the new administration can see that the world has changed. America is emerging from the guilt and reticence of the Vietnam period into a new era of international relations—a difficult time in which *détente* is no longer the order of the day and SALT negotiations are purely hypothetical.

Certainly President Carter's foreign policy was not mediocre. For the first time in three decades the West embarked on an ideological crusade, brandishing the banner of human rights. In the Middle East, Egypt's about-face led to the Camp David talks—and to an Israeli-Egyptian agreement whose limitations do not outweigh its psychological or political significance. And Carter was able to reinforce American ties with China, and the United States showed a new face in Africa and Latin America, reaching hopeful, if only provisional, compromises in the Panama Canal Zone, Zimbabwe, and Nicaragua.

By comparison, Reagan's decision to try a "big stick" policy in El Salvador was clearly a step backward—a shortsighted policy that can only damage long-term United States interests in Latin America by strengthening the unpopular, corrupt, and conservative social forces that even now are one of the biggest obstacles to effective economic development. Such shortsighted policies are more dangerous than ever. Without being apocalyptic, we must recognize that crisis is imminent in many countries of the Third World, where economic stagnation, demographic growth, and social inequality will undoubtedly mean upheaval in the coming decade.

If the United States and Western Europe want to avoid a global crisis caused by these imbalances in the Third World, they must seriously reconsider their policy toward underdeveloped countries. They must encourage political movements dedicated to structural reform. They must help to introduce economic efficiency and, even more important, social justice.

And they will find that such a policy is not in essence inconsistent with the fundamental interests of the West. Certainly, at least, it is not shortsighted.

But the West cannot pursue a reformist policy in the Third World unless, at the same time, it is prepared vigorously to challenge the Soviet Union whenever and wherever that it necessary. The error in Carter's foreign policy was its naïveté, its underestimation of the Soviets and their intentions. To pretend that arms limitation is the only, or even the most important, dimension of relations between the United States and the U.S.S.R. is to ignore crucial political strategic factors in the East-West conflict. After all, as the Russians never tire of demonstrating, national security is hardly their only strategic goal.

During the years between 1975 and 1980, the Soviet Union played its hand with calculated audacity, taking full advantage of its military power and the political impotence of the United States. All the "blanks" have been filled, every opportunity seized. And while Western experts waste their time pondering each Soviet success, trying to decide if it is part of a global strategy or merely an opportunistic coup, the U.S.S.R. goes on to score yet other victories in Africa and Asia whenever it has the chance. Certainly it is hard to imagine that the U.S.S.R. will now lay down its hand, although it may also turn to less direct strategies, since it has to cope with Afghanistan and also re-establish some kind of law and order in Poland.

We may not be reviving the cold war, but clearly the era of *détente* is gone. The Russians' recent breakthroughs in Afghanistan and elsewhere, their increased nuclear potential, the new Republican administration in Washington, and the global crisis—all this marks the beginning of a new era based on open competition and antagonism between East and West.

Although perhaps not hostage to *détente*, Western Europe now finds that it is trapped in ambiguity, for while many Europeans feel that they owe their security to the real or imagined protection of American nuclear forces, they also maintain excellent relations with the Soviet Union—relations based on an assumption of relative European neutrality. How long can they maintain this precarious balance? Certainly, whatever policies are adopted in the future, it is imperative that Europeans recognize their unstable position. Yet many European political leaders have tried to disguise this danger in order to reassure the public—and thus ensure their own re-election. Such bad faith can only harm them in the end.

The problem is no longer, as it was for Nixon and Kissinger, to create a new international balance. The task today is to mend the gaping holes in the old order, to prepare responses to both existing and imminent crises. The West must acquire the military means to intervene in the Middle East if that should become necessary, and the United States and Europe must also give considerable effort to restoring a more favorable balance of power in the Persian Gulf. The Soviet regime faces serious problems in Poland, Afghanistan, and at home, where a weak economy and dissatisfied consumers threaten to undermine its foreign policies. And yet the Russians' own growing military power may well encourage them to intervene even in the European theater. Although this is an improbable course of action, it is not an impossible one. Certainly, the U.S.S.R. has demonstrated its desire for a strategic base in western Asia.

The Soviet invasion of Afghanistan was not an end in itself. It was, rather, an early phase in a long military and diplomatic contest that will undoubtedly renew itself every time an opportunity arises.

Soviet military superiority—in both conventional and nuclear warfare—is already an established fact. Whatever steps America now takes to regain an advantage in the arms race, the U.S.S.R. is likely to maintain its lead during the next few years—until 1985 at least. And it would be surprising if it did not seek to take advantage of this lead, even if that means taking some calculated risks. That is why the Soviet Union's military power is today the principal problem in international relations.

Looking ahead to the end of the next decade, few people seriously question the West's ability to adapt to imminent technical and cultural changes. But in the meantime, all sorts of crises and confrontations are possible. Comforted by an illusion of security and by the false assurances of their politicians, Westerners could hardly be less prepared to meet the psychological challenge.

In spite of its extraordinary military development in both space and naval technology, the U.S.S.R. also faces serious problems, particularly in Poland. Whatever the outcome—and it will undoubtedly be dramatic—what has happened in Poland since 1980 is an historical turning point. Nothing of such importance has happened since the stabilization of Eastern Europe in 1948.

The Soviet Union cannot at once maintain its aggressive military policy and respond to domestic demands for economic progress. In this sense, a costly military engagement in Afghanistan would undoubtedly cause problems for the Soviet regime. Knowing this, it seems either cowardly or willfully blind not to aid the Afghan resistance. One has only to recall how costly the Vietnam war was in the end for the United States. Nevertheless, it is unlikely that Russia will allow itself to become mired in Afghanistan. Certainly it will not hesitate to strike forcefully if that becomes necessary, without gradual escalation. Nor will there be Soviet military retreat: a withdrawal would gain little favor from the West, and it is very important for the U.S.S.R. not to give the appearance of defeat. The Soviets plan to stay in Afghanistan as long as it is necessary to transform it into a vassal state comparable to Outer Mongolia. But the West could make this occupation considerably more costly than it has been so far. The intervention in Afghanistan was not a backyard maneuver of little concern to anyone but the Soviets and the Afghans themselves. Unless it is eclipsed by an even more serious crisis, closer to the Western theater, it will almost certainly be a major international sore spot for the years to come.

CHRONOLOGY

1. From Afghan Monarchy to Buffer State

1747	Pushtuns create an Afghan monarchy.
1747–1773	Reign of Ahmad Shah Durani.
1773–1793	Timor Shah.
1793–1826	Time of internal trouble and erosion of monarch's power.
1826–1863	Dost Mohammad.
1839–1842	First Anglo-Afghan war. British defeat.
1855	Anglo-Afghan treaty. First British attempt to create a buffer state between their empire and Tsarist Russia.
1864–1879	Sher Ali Khan.
1878	Second Anglo-Afghan war. Early losses, but eventual victory for the British.

2. The Creation of Modern Afghanistan

1880–1901	Abdur Rahman Khan, founder of the modern Afghan state, attempts to centralize the state. Suppresses rebellious regions including

	Hazarajat and forces Islamization of Kafiri-stan.
1893	Creation of the Durand line which today marks the border between Afghanistan and Pakistan.
1901–1919	Habibullah.
1919–1929	Amanullah. Third Anglo-Afghan war in 1919 gave Afghanistan complete control of its foreign policy. Treaty of Friendship with the U.S.S.R. in 1920. Country open to foreign visitors. Failure of a series of administrative and social reforms.
1926	Treaty of Neutrality and Nonaggression with the Soviet Union.
1929	Bacha-i Saqao, a Tajik and the son of a water seller, seizes Kabul and proclaims himself king. He is executed after ruling nine months.
1929–1933	Nadir Shah. Restoration of Pushtun control of the government.
1931	First constitution. New Soviet-Afghan Treaty of Neutrality and Nonaggression.
1933–1973	Zahir Shah. The King's uncles control the state until 1949.
1946	First American economic aid to Afghanistan. Renewal of a Treaty of Friendship with the Soviet Union.
1947	India achieves independence. Pakistan proclaims a constitution. Afghanistan first confronts the problem of "Pushtunistan."
1953–1963	Decade dominated by the King's cousin, Prince Daud, who acts as Prime Minister. Five-year plans: 1956–61 and 1962–67. Technical cooperation with both the Soviet Union and the United States. Soviet aid increases

	considerably after 1954, amounting to $700 million between 1954 and 1968. This aid represents two-thirds of all foreign aid to Afghanistan. American aid totals $526 million between 1946 and 1978.
1954	The United States refuses to sell arms to Afghanistan.
1955	Khrushchev and Bulganin visit Kabul. Treaty of Neutrality and Nonaggression extended for ten years.
1960	Khrushchev visits Kabul.
1963	Brezhnev visits Kabul.
1964–1965	New liberal constitution. Soviet Union builds the Kabul-Charikar-Doschi road, running a tunnel under the Salang Pass.
1967	Afghanistan and the Soviet Union sign protocol guaranteeing delivery of Afghan natural gas from 1967 to 1985.
1968	Beginning of student demonstrations in Kabul. Unrest lasts until 1972.
1971–1973	Economic stagnation, drought, and famine.
July 17, 1973	*Coup d'état.* Daud proclaims republic.
1974	Daud moves closer to Iran and Saudi Arabia and tries to improve relations with Pakistan.
1975	Podgorny visits Kabul and extends Soviet-Afghan Treaty of Neutrality and Nonaggression for another ten years. Agreements made with Iran include a $700 million loan.
1977	Daud visits Moscow. Thirty-year commercial agreement made with the Soviet Union.
1977–1978	Drought and famine.

3. The New Regime

April 24, 1978	Daud overthrown and executed.
April 30	Democratic republic of Afghanistan pro-

	claimed and recognized by the Soviet Union.
May 15	Tass announces that the Soviet Union is taking charge of Afghan security forces.
July 12	Decree 6 abolishes usury and peasants' debts.
July	The Khalq faction ousts members of rival Parcham faction from key posts.
August– September	Regime arrests many senior officers and several ministers, including the Minister of Defense, Abdul Qadar.
October	Decree 7 guarantees women's rights.
November 28	Decree 8 announces agrarian reforms to take effect on January 1, 1979.
December	Taraki visits Moscow, where he signs a treaty guaranteeing friendship and cooperation for a period of twenty years.
January 16, 1979	The Shah flees from Iran. The Islamic revolution spreads throughout country within a month.
February 14	The United States Ambassador in Kabul is kidnapped and killed during a raid by Afghan security forces.
March	A mutiny of troops stationed in Herat is supported by the people. More than twenty Russians are killed during an uprising. Hafizullah Amin is named Prime Minister. The insurrection that began during the winter in Nuristan and Hazarajat spreads throughout several other provinces.
April–August	Large numbers of soldiers and officers desert from the Afghan army. Afghan refugees begin to pour into Pakistan.
July 27	Hafizullah Amin becomes Minister of Defense and Minister of the Interior.

August 5	Regime crushes a military uprising in Kabul led by the Bala Hissar garrison.
September 16	Hafizullah Amin becomes President of the Republic and Secretary General of the ruling party, the DPPA.
October 14	Mutiny of troops at Kishkur base in Kabul.
October–December	Hafizullah Amin announces concessions and releases political prisoners but also orders increased repression by military.
December 25	Beginning of Soviet military intervention.
December 27	Soviet troops occupy Kabul.

4. Afghanistan under Soviet Occupation

December 27, 1979	Brezhnev congratulates Babrak Karmal, new President of the Republic and Secretary General of the DPPA.
January 6, 1980	Several thousand political prisoners are freed.
January 11	A new government is formed and includes members of both the Khalq and Parcham factions.
January 13	Brezhnev declares that the Soviet intervention was a response to appeal by friendly government and was intended to counter interference by foreign powers.
January 29	Representatives from thirty-six Muslim countries meet in Islamabad, vote by an overwhelming majority to condemn the Soviet intervention in Afghanistan.
February 21	A strike in the bazaar in Kabul protests Soviet occupation.
February 22	Martial law is proclaimed in Kabul.
March 1	Offensive by Soviet and Afghan troops in Kunar province.

Mid-March	Offensive in Paktia province.
March 28	New anti-Soviet demonstrations in Kabul.
April 25–30	Anniversary of the revolution that led to the creation of the Afghan republic. Demonstrations in Kabul are fiercely suppressed.
End of May	New offensives in Kunar and the Ghazni region.
May–June	Demonstrations in Kabul against the regime. Demonstrations in Mazar-i-Sharif and Herat.
September	Soviet offensive in the Panjir valley and Kunar province.
End of December	Mutiny of police officers in Kabul. Demonstrations and acts of sabotage mark the first anniversary of Soviet occupation.
January 12–14, 1981	Sabotage continues in Kabul.
January 24	Muslim states meeting in Taef, Saudi Arabia, modify their condemnation of the Soviet intervention in Afghanistan.
March 9	President Reagan declares that he is prepared to send arms to the members of the Afghan resistance.
March 11	The United Nations High Commission on Refugees declares in Geneva that there are more than two million Afghan refugees in Pakistan.*
March 27	The President of Pakistan states that the Afghan resistance movement should receive "durable and certain" aid, but that "the sanctuary must first be strengthened."

---

* This figure includes 1,673,000 officially registered refugees, approximately 300,-000 that have not been entered on official rolls, and some 80,000 nomads. Among the total number in Pakistan, 1,310,000 are in the Northwest Province and 335,000 are in Baluchistan. According to Teheran, there are also 250,000 Afghan refugees in Iran.

End of March	Washington prepares a plan for aid to Pakistan amounting to $500 million during the next two years.
May	Soviet offensive in Kandahar province.
September	Soviet offensive in Panjir valley.

ANNOTATED BIBLIOGRAPHY

Donald N. Wilbur, *An Annotated Bibliography of Afghanistan,*
Third Edition (New York: Taplinger, 1968). The most recent and complete bibliography.

Among nineteenth-century travelers:

M. Elphinstone, *An Account of the Kingdom of Cabul* (London, 1815). Describes all aspects of the country and its inhabitants, both north and south of the Hindu-Kush.

A. Burnes, *Voyages à l'embouchure de l'Indus à Lahore, Caboul, Belkh et à Boukhara et retour par la Perse, pendant les
années 1831 et 1833,* four volumes (Paris, 1835).

C. Masson, *Narrative of Various Journeys in Baluchistan,
Afghanistan and the Pundjab,* three volumes (London,
1842). Fourth volume published in 1844.

G. Robertson, *The Kafirs of the Hindu-Kush* (London, 1900).
An exciting ethnological report and the classic work on
Nuristan. It also treats the Kafir country in Pakistan.

Among the major general works on Afghanistan,
the following must not be omitted:

W. K. Frazer-Tytler, *Afghanistan,* Third Edition revised by
M. Gillett (Oxford: Oxford University Press, 1967). A pio-
neering work, first published in 1953.

M. Klimburg, *Afghanistan, Das Land in historische span-
nungsfeld Mittelasiens* (Vienna, 1966).

Donald N. Wilbur (ed.), *Afghanistan,* Second Edition (New
York: Taplinger, 1962). An excellent introduction by a
scholar of Iran.

Louis Dupree, *Afghanistan,* Third Edition (Princeton, N.J.:
Princeton University Press, 1980). The most easily accessi-
ble work in this category and the most recent, it offers a
very good introduction to the past as well as the present.

Olaf Caroe, *The Pathans* (London: Macmillan, 1965). The
major work on the Pushtun people, in Afghanistan and
Pakistan.

E. Bacon, "An Inquiry into the History of the Hazara Mon-
gols of Afghanistan," in *Southwestern Journal of Anthropol-
ogy,* 7 (1951), pp. 230–247. Offers a valuable contribution
on the Hazara people.

Vartan Gregorian, *The Emergence of Modern Afghanistan*
(Stanford: Stanford University Press, 1969). The best book
on the modern period, it covers the history of the country
from 1880 to the end of World War II with great accuracy
and clarity. It also includes an extensive bibliography.

R. Akhramovich, *Outline History of Afghanistan after the Second World War* (Moscow, 1966). I have not been able to
find a copy of this book, but it is said to be a useful work.

The Area Handbook of Afghanistan, Washington, D.C. Useful, particularly for changes in recent years and for statistics. It appeared throughout the 1960s and 1970s until 1975.

*On the Soviet Union and general questions of
nationalism and colonialism in this region:*
D. Boersner, *The Bolsheviks and the National and Colonial
Question 1917–1928* (Geneva: Droz, 1957).

*On the Soviet Union and its relations
with the Muslim peoples of Central Asia,
the most important contributions include:*
E. Allworth (ed.), *The Nationality Question in Soviet Central
Asia* (New York: Praeger, 1973); and by the same author,
Central Asia: A Century of Russian Rule (New York: Co-
lumbia University Press, 1967).
H. Carrère d'Encausse and S. Schram, *Le Marxisme et l'Asie
1853–1964* (Paris: Armand Colin, 1965). Outlines in a precise way the historical and ideological settings of the different phases of the Marxist advance in Asia.
A. Bennigsen and Ch. Lemercier-Quelquejay, *L'Islam en
l'Union soviétique* (Paris: Payot, 1968). Shows how Soviet
control was extended over Central Asia.
A. Bennigsen and Ch. Lemercier-Quelquejay, *Les Mouve-
ments nationaux chez les musulmans de Russie: le Sultanga-
lievisme au Tartaristan* (Paris: Mouton, 1960).
A. Bennigsen and S. E. Winbush, *Muslim Communism in the
Soviet Union. A Revolutionary Strategy for the Colonial
World* (Chicago: University of Chicago Press, 1979).
H. Carrère d'Encausse, *Réforme et révolution chez les musulmans de l'Empire russe, Bukhara 1867–1924* (Paris: Armand
Colin, 1966). A study of how the emirate was conquered by
the tsars and annexed by the Soviet Union.

On the Basmachi movement

Joseph Castagne, *Les Basmatchis* (Paris: E. Leroux, 1925).

Martha L. Brill, *The Basmatchi Movement*, Ph.d. dissertation, University of Paris, 1975–76, 76 pages.

See also the following article:

A. Bennigsen and Ch. Lemercier-Quelquejay, "L'Expérience soviétique en pays musulman: les leçons du passé et l'Afghanistan," in *Politique étrangère* (Paris, July 1980).

Works concerning Afghanistan since April 1978:

Fred Halliday, "Revolution in Afghanistan," in *New Left Review,* London, No. 112, November–December 1978, and "War and Revolution in Afghanistan," in *New Left Review,* No. 119, January–February 1980. Two studies, well documented by historical research, by a Marxist who is very familiar with political problems of the Third World. Fred Halliday supports the modernization program of the DPPA but also offers a critical assessment of the Khalq regime.

See also:

Hannah Negaran, "The Afghan Coup of April 1978: Revolution and International Security," in *Orbis,* Spring 1979.

Louis Dupree, "Afghanistan under the Khalq," in *Problems of Communism,* July–August 1979. Strongly opposes the new Afghan regime, as do

Richard S. Newall, "Revolution and Revolt in Afghanistan," in *The World Today,* London, November 1979 and David Cheffetz, "Afghanistan in Turmoil," in *International Affairs,* January 1980.

See also two excellent contributions in *Survival,* London, Vol. XXII, July–August 1980:

William E. Griffith, "Super-Power Relations after Afghanistan."

Zamay Khalilzad, "Afghanistan and the Crisis in American Foreign Policy."

The most interesting contributions in French are:
Jean-José Puig, "La Résistance afghane" (Unpublished, 1981).

Olivier Roy, "Afghanistan: la révolution par le vide," in *Esprit,* May 1980; and "Afghanistan. La guerre des paysans," in *Les révoltes logiques,* No. 13, Winter 1980–81. Two fine studies perceptive of complex Afghan realities and without *a priori* ideology.

H. Carrère d'Encausse, "Le Probleme extérieur de l'URSS et la crise afghane," in *Politique étrangère,* June 1980.

See also the special issue of *Tempes modernes,* Nos. 408–9, July–August 1980, which contains a series of excellent articles by J.-J. Puig, Mike Barry, P. Gentelle, J. Bertolino, among others. A very good special issue of the review *Herodote,* edited by Yves Lacoste, was dedicated to Afghanistan and Iran: "Pointes chauds," No. 16, Summer 1980.

Other works about Afghanistan:
F. Missen, *Le Syndrome de Kaboul* (Paris, 1979). A somewhat mediocre account.

Franceschi, *Ils ont choisi la liberté. La guerre d'Afghanistan* (Paris: Éditions arthaud, 1981), with photographs by Franceschi and P. Manoukian. A lively and well-observed journalistic account that captures the spirit of the Afghan rebels.

Two works on the condition of women:
Simone Bailleau-Lajoinie, *Condition des femmes en Afghanistan* (Paris: Éditions sociales, 1980).

Isabelle Delloye, *Des femmes d'Afghanistan* (Paris: Éditions des femmes, 1980).

Works not in French or currently in press:

John C. Griffith, *Afghanistan: Key to a Continent* (London, in press). A good introduction recounting the history of Afghanistan up to the Soviet intervention.

Bundesinstitut für Ostwissenschaftliche und Internationale Studien, *Die sowjetische Intervention in Afghanistan,* edited by Heinrich Vogel (Baden-Baden: Nomos Verlagsgesellschaft, 1980). A most important work, which contains ten articles centering on the foreign aspects of the Afghan conflict: Russian expansion in the nineteenth century; Soviet expansion in the twentieth century; problems of Islam; causes of the intervention; regional consequences of the intervention; reactions to the intervention among the Warsaw Pact signatories, in the United States, in Western Europe, and in the Third World; Afghanistan as a test of Soviet political and military doctrines. See in particular the article by Wolfgang Berner about the lessons and prospects of the events in Afghanistan in 1978–80: "Der Kampf um Kaboul," pp. 319–65.

INDEX

Afghanistan 2, 5–6, 11; agrarian reform in, 36–37, 48; border conditions, 3–4, 5, 62; British agents in, 2–3; British attempts to colonize, 14, 15; as buffer state, 10; climatic conditions in, 15–16; communists in, 9; *coup d'état* of April 1978, 19, 20, 34, 55, 75; crafts of, 2; cultural influences in, 13; Daud government, 28–30; Democratic Republic of Afghanistan government, 34; diet, 5–6; ethnic groups of, 16; exports of, 30; farming in, 22; folk tales, 18; foreign policy, 26–27; government bureaucracy, 29, 31; history of, 13–15; industrial working class, 20; irrigation of land, 16, 21, 23, 37; Khalq faction government, 9, 32, 33, 35, 36–38, 40, 41, 42, 43, 44–46, 47, 48, 55, 56, 57; King Zahir government, 27–28; landowners, 21, 22–23, 24, 36–37; land reform, 24, 46; left-wing groups in, 31; life expectancy in, 21; literacy campaign, 38, 46; Marxist regime of, 24; middle class, 44–45; mujahedeen, 5, 6; nomads, 20; Persian culture, 13–14; poetry, 18; population of, 20, 22; poverty in, 20, 23–24, 46; refugees from, 64; resistance organizations in exile, 1, 3, 4, 9, 47–61; Soviet advisers in, 43; Soviet invasion of, 8, 14, 25, 43, 47–61, 62–72, 73–91; and Soviet Union, 26–27; terrain of, 15–16; trading partners of, 30; transportation within, 19; treaties, 26, 27, 38; tribal alliances, 65; tribal headmen, 21, 23, 25–26, 37–38; tribal societies, 19; village communities, 22; women's rights in, 35, 36, 38, 49

Afghan Milli. *See* National Islamic Revolution of the Afghan People

107